Reading and Writing Sourcebook

Authors

Ruth Nathan
Laura Robb

Great Source Education Group
a Houghton Mifflin Company

Authors

Ruth Nathan one of the authors of *Writers Express* and *Write Away*, is the author of many professional books and articles on literacy. She earned a Ph.D. in reading from Oakland University in Rochester, Michigan, where she co-headed their reading research laboratory for several years. She currently teaches in third grade, as well as consults with numerous schools and organizations on reading.

Laura Robb author of *Reading Strategies That Work* and *Teaching Reading in the Middle School*, has taught language arts at Powhatan School in Boyce, Virginia, for more than thirty years. She also mentors and coaches teachers in Virginia public schools and speaks at conferences throughout the country.

Contributing Writer

Anina Robb is a writer and a teacher. She earned an MFA in Poetry from Sarah Lawrence College and an MA in English from Hollins College. Ms. Robb taught English for four years in public schools in New York City.

Printed in the United States of America.

International Standard Book Number: 0-669-48436-9

4 5 6 7 8 9 10 — RRDW — 07 06 05 04 03

Table of Contents

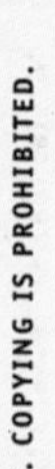

Be an Active Reader

When you read, do you mark up the text? Do you write down questions about your reading? Active readers read with a pen or pencil in hand. They make notes, underline, and draw.

Read 4 poems and see the examples of how an active reader took notes. You too can **draw, question, make clear,** and **connect** to the reading.

DRAW

You can **draw** to help you "see" what you read. Here the reader has drawn a shooting star. The picture puts an image with the words in the poem.

Response Notes

"Shooting Stars"
by Aileen Fisher

When stars get loosened
in their sockets,
they shoot off through
the night like rockets.
But though I stay
and watch their trip
and search where they
have seemed to slip,
I never yet have found a CHIP
to carry in my pockets.

sockets (sock•ets)—hollow openings into which something, such as an eye, fits.
rockets (rock•ets)—flying machines that travel through space.

II. QUESTION

You can ask **questions** as you read. Asking questions—and trying to answer them—as you read helps you understand what you're reading.

"First Moon Landing"
by J. Patrick Lewis

Response Notes

Two highfliers,
Buzz and Neil,
Said they couldn't
Wait to feel
Just what kind of
Moon it was—
"Take a look around,"
Said Buzz.
Open the hatch
And out the door,
Down the ladder
To the moonlit floor.
After he had
Sunk his heel
Into the dusty
Ocean, Neil
Knew what a lovely
Moon it was—
"One *small step . . ."*
Said Neil to Buzz.

What kind of moon is it?

MAKE CLEAR

You can **make clear** what you read by circling, underlining, or highlighting certain parts and writing notes. That way you know what is happening in the reading. Here the notes remind the reader. They make it clear that the moon is really dark and cold, even though it looks bright.

Response Notes

moon = cold
and dark

"The Moon" by Lillian M. Fisher

The moon has no light
of its own.
It's cold and dark
and dead as stone,
But it catches light
from the burning sun
And shows itself
When each day is done.

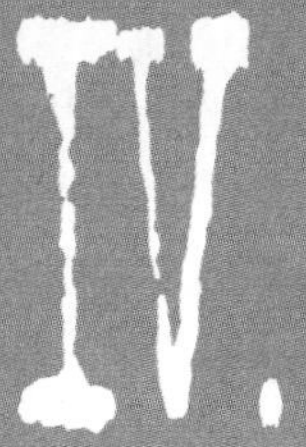

IV. CONNECT

As you read, think about what the reading means to you. **Connect** to it. How does the reading make you feel? How is it like something you know? What do you think about it? Here the poem is about the joy of song. How has the reader connected his or her feelings to the poem?

"Song" by Ashley Bryan

Response Notes

Sing to the sun
It will listen
And warm your words
Your joy will rise
Like the sun
And glow
Within you
Sing to the moon
It will hear
And soothe your cares
Your fears will set
Like the moon
And fade
Within you

Singing always makes me happy, too!

How to Read a Lesson

Here are 3 easy steps to help you get the most out of the readings in this book.

1. For each reading, **read it once** and just circle or underline the important parts.
2. Then **read it again**. On the second reading, write questions or comments in the Notes.
3. Then, at the end of each reading, you will find a part called **Reread**. This part asks you to go back one more time and be sure you have answered all the questions.

Red=Follow Directions

Blue=Write Here

Black=Read This

PLAY BALL, AMELIA BEDELIA

II. READ

Read this part of the book *Play Ball, Amelia Bedelia*.

1. First, read and circle parts that make you wonder if Amelia Bedelia can help the Grizzlies win.
2. Then, read the story again. Write in the Notes any **questions** that pop into your head.

Play Ball, Amelia Bedelia
by Peggy Parish

The game was not going well for the Grizzlies. The score was Tornados 8, Grizzlies 5. The Grizzlies were at bat. It was the last inning.

They had two outs. The bases were loaded. And Amelia Bedelia was at bat. The Grizzlies were worried.

Response Notes

EXAMPLE:
What will happen when Amelia bats?

at bat—having a turn at hitting in baseball.
inning (in•ning)—part of a baseball game when each team comes to bat.
outs—plays that stop a runner or hitter from continuing to play. Each team has three outs each time a team is at bat.
loaded (load•ed)—full. A player was on each of the three bases.
worried (wor•ried)—nervous; uneasy.

1

By reading and rereading, you will do what good readers do.

reread

Read the story again. Look for details that help you understand how Amelia Bedelia helped her team. Be sure you answered the **Stop and Retell** questions.

1

Play Ball, Amelia Bedelia

Would you want to play in a game that was new to you? Amelia Bedelia doesn't mind. She plays in a baseball game, but she doesn't know anything about baseball. How does Amelia Bedelia help her team?

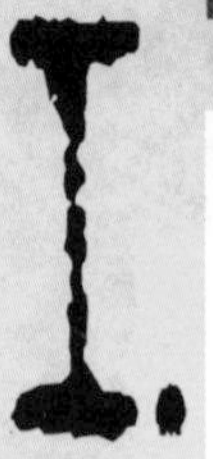

BEFORE YOU READ

When you think about what will happen next in a story, you are predicting.

1. Look at the pictures. Read the title and the first sentence.
2. Then fill out the chart.

CLUE	PREDICTION
Predicting Clue #1 **Title**	I think the story will show how Amelia Bedelia plays baseball.
Predicting Clue #2 **Pictures**	
Predicting Clue #3 **First Sentence**	

MY PURPOSE

How does Amelia Bedelia help the Grizzlies play ball?

READ

Read this part of the book *Play Ball, Amelia Bedelia*.

1. First, read and circle parts that make you wonder if Amelia Bedelia can help the Grizzlies win.
2. Then, read the story again. Write in the Notes any **questions** that pop into your head.

Play Ball, Amelia Bedelia

by Peggy Parish

The game was not going well for the Grizzlies. The score was Tornados 8, Grizzlies 5. The Grizzlies were at bat. It was the last inning.

They had two outs. The bases were loaded. And Amelia Bedelia was at bat. The Grizzlies were worried.

Response Notes

EXAMPLE:

What will happen when Amelia bats?

at bat—having a turn at hitting in baseball.
inning (in•ning)—part of a baseball game when each team comes to bat.
outs—plays that stop a runner or hitter from continuing to play. Each team has three outs each time a team is at bat.
loaded (load•ed)—full. A player was on each of the three bases.
worried (wor•ried)—nervous; uneasy.

"Please, Amelia Bedelia," they said. "Please hit that ball hard."

Amelia Bedelia swung at the first ball. She missed.

She swung at the second ball. And again she missed.

"Please, Amelia Bedelia, please," shouted the Grizzlies.

Amelia Bedelia swung at the next ball. And oh, how she hit that ball!

STOP AND RETELL **stop and retell** STOP AND RETELL

What do you remember about Amelia Bedelia so far?

STOP AND RETELL STOP AND RETELL

"Run, Amelia Bedelia, run!" yelled the boys. "Run to first base." And Amelia Bedelia ran.

PLAY BALL, AMELIA BEDELIA (continued)

Response Notes

"Tom says stealing is all right," she said, "so I'll just steal all the bases. I will make sure the Grizzlies win." Amelia Bedelia scooped up first base, and second base, and third base.

"Home!" shouted the boys. "Run home, Amelia Bedelia!"

STOP AND RETELL stop and retell STOP AND RETELL

What is the story about?

STOP AND RETELL STOP AND RETELL STOP AND RETELL

Amelia Bedelia looked puzzled, but she did not stop running. And on her way she scooped up home plate too. The boys were too surprised to say a thing. Then Tom yelled, "We won! We won the game!"

stealing (steal•ing)—running ahead to the next base.
scooped—picked.
Home—the last base where one scores.
puzzled (puz•zled)—confused.

Response Notes

"Amelia Bedelia, come back!" shouted the boys. "We won!" But Amelia Bedelia was running too fast to hear. She did not stop until she <u>reached</u> home.

"That is a silly game," she said. "Having me run all the way home!" <u>Suddenly</u> she heard a loud roar.

"Hurray! Hurray! Hurray for Amelia Bedelia!" There were the Grizzlies.

"We won! The score was Grizzlies 9, Tornados 8," said Jimmy. "You saved the game, Amelia Bedelia."

"I'm glad I could help you boys out," said Amelia Bedelia.

reached—got.
Suddenly (sud•den•ly**)**—quickly; without warning.

reread

Read the story again. Look for details that help you understand how Amelia Bedelia helped her team. Be sure you answered the **Stop and Retell** questions.

WORD WORK

Missed, *missing*, and *misses* have something in common. Each word has a **base word** (*miss*) and an **ending** *(-ed, -ing, -es*). An ending added to a base word is called a **suffix** (suh-fix).

Amelia *missed* the ball!
Amelia is *missing* the ball!
Amelia *misses* the ball!

One way to add a suffix to a base word is just to add it.

miss	+	ed	=	*missed*
miss	+	ing	=	*missing*
miss	+	es	=	*misses*

A suffix is a great tool for making new words. Add the suffixes to the words below to make new words.

jump + ing =

leap + ed =

read + ing =

mix + es =

spend + ing =

wait + ing =

smell + ed=

READING REMINDER

Stories show what characters are like by what they say and do.

GET READY TO WRITE

A. MAKE A LIST

Pretend you are writing a letter to a friend. Tell your friend about the funny things Amelia Bedelia did. Brainstorm a list of what you want to include below. One idea is on the list. You fill in the rest.

1. She took the first base.
2.
3.
4.

B. LOOK AT A MODEL

Look at these 5 parts of a friendly letter.

1. date → September 10, 2000

2. greeting → Dear Jim,

3. body → Today I saw a strange ball game. Amelia Bedelia played in it, and she was funny. She stole the bases!

4. closing → Your friend,

5. signature → Jill

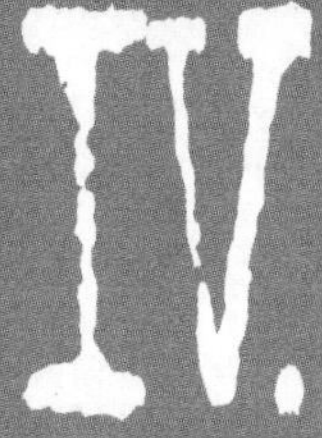

WRITE

Now you are ready to write your own **letter**.

1. Use the ideas from your brainstorming list on page 18.
2. First, check the 3 ideas you want to include.
3. Follow the 5 parts of a friendly letter.
4. Use the Writers' Checklist to edit your work.

Continue your letter on the next page.

Continue your letter.

WRITERS' CHECKLIST

Commas

☐ **Did you use commas correctly in the heading, greeting, and closing?**

EXAMPLES:

Bedford, Iowa
Dear Susan,
Your friend,

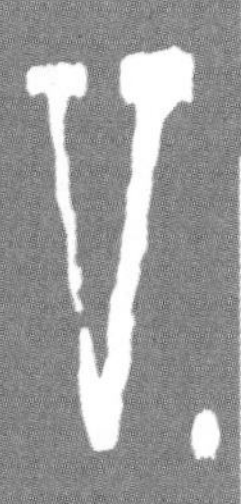

LOOK BACK

Write an answer to this question. What part of the story about Amelia Bedelia did you enjoy the most?

Think about Your Reading

READERS' CHECKLIST

Enjoyment

☐ **Did you like the reading?**

☐ **Would you recommend the reading to a friend?**

2

Poems About the Weather

How do you feel on a rainy day? How do you feel on a sunny day? Do you enjoy snow, wind, and fog? Talk to your reading partner about the kind of weather you like.

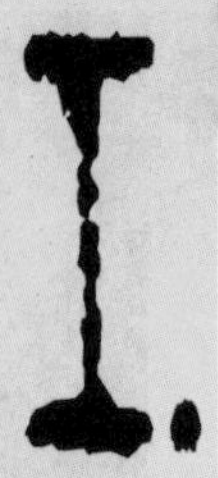

BEFORE YOU READ

Say the word *weather* to yourself. What other words pop into your mind?

1. Use the words you came up with in a web.
2. Fill in the Word Web below.
3. Write as many words or phrases that relate to weather as you can.

weather

MY PURPOSE

What do the poems tell about weather?

II. READ

Read the 3 poems once to yourself.

1. Then, read the poems out loud to a reading partner. As your partner reads, circle the weather words.
2. Read the poems again and, in the Notes, **draw** a picture that goes with some words you have circled.

"Winter Morning" by Ogden Nash

Winter is the king of showmen,
Turning tree stumps into snow men
And houses into birthday cakes
And spreading sugar over lakes.
Smooth and clean and frosty white
The world looks good enough to bite.
That's the season to be young,
Catching snowflakes on your tongue.

Snow is snowy when it's snowing,
I'm sorry it's slushy when it's going.

Response Notes

EXAMPLE:

DOUBLE-ENTRY JOURNAL

Quote	What You Think This Means
"The world looks good enough to bite."	

showmen (show•men)—people who act for others.
spreading (spread•ing)—putting some, or a layer, on.
frosty (frost•y)—freezing and shiny.
slushy (slush•y)—full of melting snow and ice.

Response Notes

"Go Wind" by Lilian Moore

Go wind, blow
Push wind, swoosh.
Shake things
take things
make things
fly.

<u>Ring</u> things
swing things
<u>fling</u> things
high.

Go wind, blow
Push things
wheee.

No, wind, no.
Not me—
not *me.*

Ring—hit things like bells so they make a loud noise.
fling—throw.

DOUBLE-ENTRY JOURNAL

Quote	What You Think This Means
"No, wind, no.	
Not me—	
Not me."	

"Mister Sun" by J. Patrick Lewis

Response Notes

Mister Sun
    Wakes up at dawn,
Puts his golden
    Slippers on,
Climbs the summer
    Sky at noon,
Trading places
    With the moon.

Trading (trad•ing)—switching.

Response Notes

Mister Sun
Runs away
With the blue tag
End of day,
Switching off the
Globe lamplight,
Pulling down the
Shades of night.

Shades—things like blinds or curtains that block off light.

DOUBLE-ENTRY JOURNAL

Quote	What You Think This Means
"Pulling down the Shades of night."	

reread

Read each poem again. Think about what the poems tell about the weather. Be sure you have answered the **Double-entry Journal** questions.

WORD WORK

If you can read one word, many times you can read a word that's almost the same.

Say *king*. Now take off the *k* and put *st* in front of *ing*. The new word is *sting*.

Use the letters in the box to build new words. We call these letters **consonants** (*f, b, m, l*) and **consonant clusters** (*sp, st, sn*).

s	t	f	b	sp	m	st	sn	sh	l

1. Make new words from 2 words below.
2. You can use letters from the box more than once. One has been done for you.

cakes bakes .... sun ....

....

....

....

....

....

READING REMINDER

Paying attention to particular words can help you understand and enjoy a poem.

GET READY TO WRITE

MAKE A CHART

Get ready to write a poem about weather. Brainstorm a list of weather words and the sounds they make.

1. Study the 2 examples.

2. Then add 3–5 words and sounds of your own.

Weather Word	Sound
hail	ding, ding
tornado	hiss

WRITE

Now you are ready to write a weather **poem**.

1. Number the weather words and sounds on page 28 in the order you want to list them.
2. Now write your poem. Give it a title.
3. Use the Writers' Checklist to edit your poem.

Title:

Continue your poem on the next page.

Continue your poem below.

WRITERS' CHECKLIST

Spelling

☐ Did you spell each word correctly? Ask a partner to read your poem and check your spelling.

V. LOOK BACK

Which weather poem was easiest to read? Which one was hardest? Write what made them easy or hard.

Think about Your Reading

READERS' CHECKLIST

Ease

☐ Was the reading easy to read?

☐ Were you able to read it smoothly?

3

Frogs

Have you ever held a frog? Have you ever heard the sound a frog makes? Sometimes you read to find out about things. What can you learn about frogs?

I. BEFORE YOU READ

Get ready to read by looking at the sentences below.

1. If you agree with a sentence, put a check. (√)

2. If you disagree with a sentence, put an X.

3. Talk about your answers with a reading partner.

✔ agree ✘ disagree

______ Frogs are born in water.

______ Baby frogs look like fish.

______ Frogs can live in water and on land.

______ Frogs come from eggs.

______ Frogs do not swim well.

MY PURPOSE

What are baby frogs like, and how do they grow?

II. READ

Read this part of the book *Frogs*.

1. First, read and underline facts about baby frogs.
2. Read *Frogs* again and write in the Notes sentences that **make clear** what you have learned about how frogs grow.

Frogs by Laura Driscoll

Ker-plunk! Something splashes into the pond.

A frog! It has strong back legs. It has webbed feet. It swims fast.

Frogs feel at home in the pond. Why? Because they begin life in the water—as tiny frog eggs. In the spring, a mother frog lays lots of eggs.

webbed—connected; part that connects the toes of certain animals.

Response Notes

EXAMPLE:

Mother frogs lay eggs.

STOP AND THINK **stop and think** STOP AND THINK

Why do frogs feel at home in ponds?

STOP AND THINK STOP AND THINK STOP AND THINK

Response Notes

Frogs (continued)

The eggs hatch. Frog babies swim out. They look like fish. They swim like fish. They even breathe underwater like fish.

But they are not fish They are tadpoles. They will grow up to be frogs.

Soon the tadpoles change. They get bigger. They grow little back legs, then front legs.

And little by little, their tails shrink and disappear!

Something also changes inside them.

hatch—come out of an egg.
shrink—get smaller.
disappear (dis•ap•**pear**)—go away.

STOP AND THINK **stop and think** STOP AND THINK

What are 2 ways the tadpole changes as it grows?

1.

2.

STOP AND THINK STOP AND THINK STOP AND THINK

FROGS (continued)

Response Notes

Now the baby frogs can breathe out of the water, like we do.

The frogs hop onto a log. They are now land animals. They still can swim. But they are not water animals anymore.

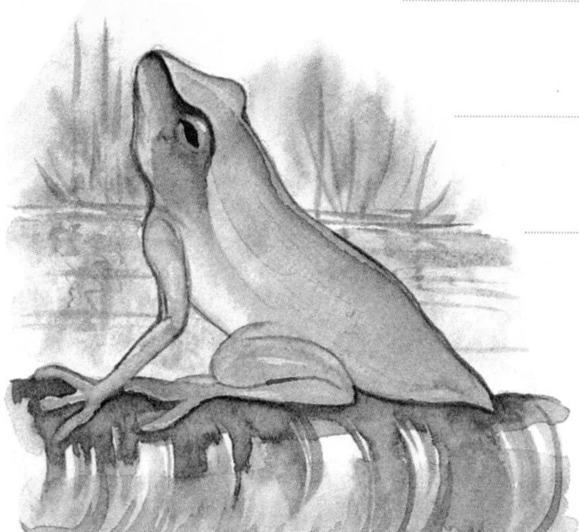

reread

Read *Frogs* again. Think about what you've learned about baby frogs and how they grow. Be sure you have answered the **Stop and Think** questions.

WORD WORK

You can make a big word by joining 2 small words. The big word is called a **compound word**.

rain + fall = *rainfall*
out + side = *outside*
tree + top = *treetop*

1. Reread *Frogs* and find 3 more compound words.
2. Write the 3 compound words below and complete the chart. One has been done for you.

Compound Word	Small Word	Small Word
1. something	some	thing
2.		
3.		
4.		

READING REMINDER

As you read, look for new facts about a subject.

III. GET READY TO WRITE

A. LIST DETAILS

Get ready to write a paragraph about how a frog grows from an egg.

1. Use the notes you wrote to help you remember key details.
2. List the details in order below.

From Egg to Frog

1.

2.

3.

4.

5.

B. LOOK AT A MODEL

A good paragraph has a beginning, middle, and end. The first sentence is called the **topic sentence**. It tells what your paragraph is going to be about.

1. For the beginning of your paragraph, choose 1 of the topic sentences below or write your own.

a. Frogs go through a lot of changes as they grow.

b. It is hard work growing up into a frog.

c. My Own:

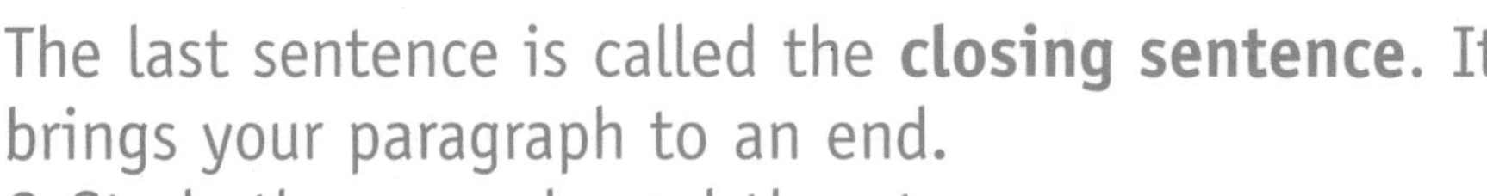

The last sentence is called the **closing sentence**. It brings your paragraph to an end.

2. Study the example and then try your own.

EXAMPLE: Frogs go through many changes as they grow up.

My Own:

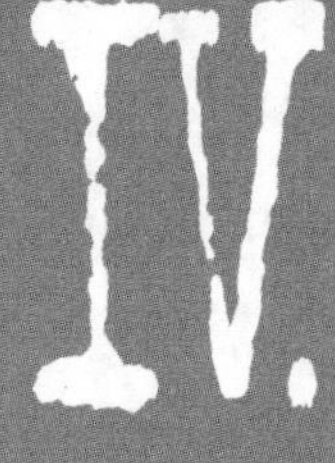

WRITE

Now write your own **paragraph**.

1. Give it a title.
2. Begin with your topic sentence.
3. Pick 3 details from page 37 to write about.
4. Finish your paragraph with your closing sentence.
5. Use the Writers' Checklist to edit your paragraph.

Title:

Continue your paragraph on the next page.

Continue your paragraph below.

WRITERS' CHECKLIST

Capitalization

☐ **Did you begin all of your sentences with a capital letter?**

EXAMPLE: *Frog babies are called tadpoles.*

V. LOOK BACK

What details about frogs can you remember? Write the details below.

Think about Your Reading

READERS' CHECKLIST

Meaning

☐ **Did you learn something from the reading?**

☐ **Did you have a strong feeling about the reading?**

4

I'll Catch the Moon

Imagine going to the moon. How would you travel there? What would you take with you? What would you miss the most?

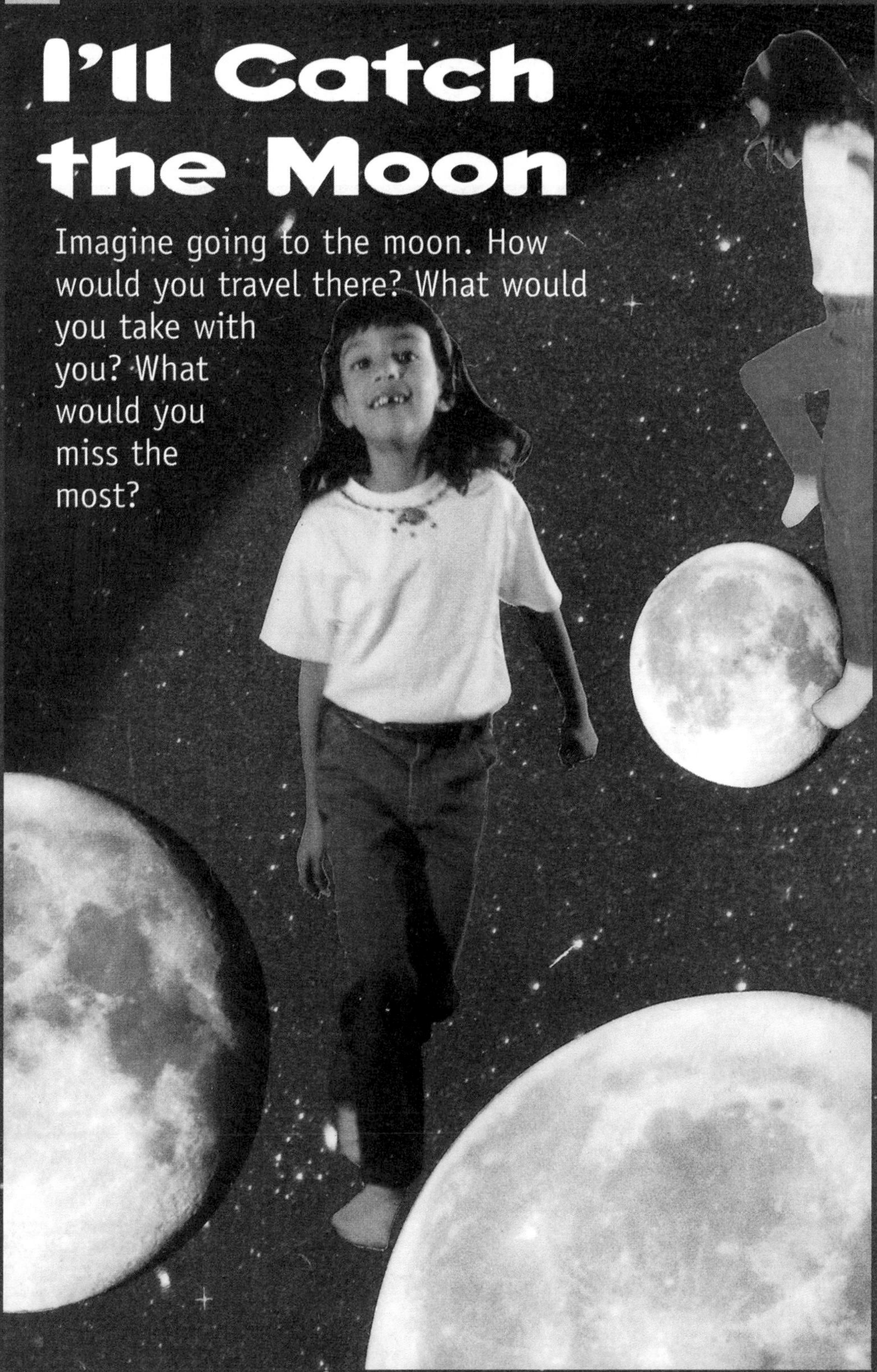

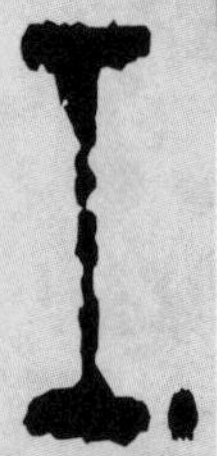

BEFORE YOU READ

When you think of the moon, what comes to mind?

1. Close your eyes and think about the moon. What do you see? What do you feel?
2. Fill in the web below. List your ideas under each heading.

What I See	What I Feel

Moon

What I Pretend	What I Know

MY PURPOSE

How can someone catch the moon?

READ

Now read *I'll Catch the Moon*.

1. Circle the parts that make pictures in your mind.
2. Then read again and **draw** in the Notes some of the pictures you see.

I'll Catch the Moon
by Nina Crews

Response Notes

Outside my window I see the city and the sky.

Honk, blink, stop, go. City moves below me.

Tall buildings climb into the air. The moon floats above.

EXAMPLE:

Moon. Silver shining like a quarter. I would like to put it in my pocket.

I've seen pictures of the moon. Men on the moon.

The man in the moon.

And a cow jumping over it. Sometimes it looks very big and sometimes very small.

floats—sits.

STOP AND THINK **stop and think** STOP AND THINK

A young girl is telling this story. What things does the girl see and feel?

STOP AND THINK STOP AND THINK STOP AND THINK

Response Notes

I'll Catch the Moon (continued)

I'd like to catch that moon. I'll build a ladder into outer space.

I'll go past buildings, past helicopters, airplanes, and clouds.

I'll climb, climb, and climb. The stars will watch me, and a comet will guide my way.

The moon and I will travel together. Round and round the world we'll go.

outer space (out•er **space)**—space outside of the Earth, where there are other planets.
helicopters (hel•i•cop•ters)—aircraft that have a propeller on top of them.
comet (com•et)—ball of dust, ice, and gasses that travels through space and looks like it has a tail.

STOP AND THINK stop and think STOP AND THINK

In your own words, predict what she will do with the moon.

STOP AND THINK STOP AND THINK STOP AND THINK

I'll Catch the Moon (continued)

Response Notes

We'll run, jump, skip, hop from night to day and day to night.

We'll play hide-and-seek in the clouds.

Then I'll go back home. My family will be missing me.

Response Notes

From my window

I'll wave to the
moon
passing above
me at night.

That's how it will be.
I think I'll go soon.

And then I'll catch the moon.

passing (pass•ing)—going by.

STOP AND THINK **stop and think** STOP AND THINK

What will the girl and moon do together?

reread

Read the story again. Notice the details of this pretend trip to catch the moon. Be sure you have answered all the **Stop and Think** questions.

WORD WORK

You have learned that you can read a word and then read another word that's almost the same.

Say *moon*. Now take off the *m* and put *sp* in front of *oon*. The new word is *spoon*.

1. Use the letters in the box to build new words. These letters are single **consonants** (such as *c, p, m*) and **consonant clusters** (such as *st, gr, scr*).

st	gr	c	sl	fr	p	scr	m	t	l	b	s	f

2. Make 3 new words from each word listed below. You will use some letters more than once.

catch	night	round
1. scratch		
2.		
3.		

READING REMINDER

Sometimes writers tell about real things that happen. Sometimes they tell about make-believe things.

GET READY TO WRITE

PREWRITE

Get ready to write a paragraph about your own pretend trip to the moon.

1. Fill in each part of the web below.
2. Talk to a reading partner about your trip.

HOW I GET THERE

-
-
-

WHAT I SEE AS I TRAVEL

-
-
-

My trip to the moon

WHAT I SEE ON THE MOON

-
-
-

WHAT I DO ON THE MOON

-
-
-

3. Write your own topic sentence that tells how you get to the moon.

Example: *I flew to the moon on an eagle's back.*

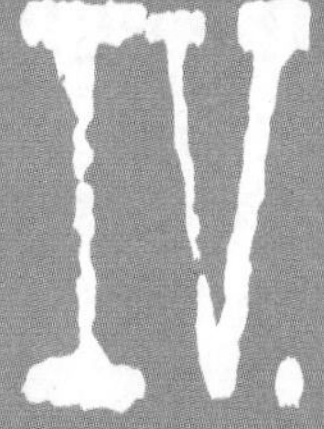

WRITE

Write a **paragraph** describing your trip to the moon. Use the ideas in your web on page 48.

1. Start with the topic sentence you wrote.
2. Write a closing sentence that tells how you felt when you came back to earth.
3. Use the Writers' Checklist to edit your description.

Title:

Continue writing your paragraph on the next page.

Continue your paragraph below.

WRITERS' CHECKLIST

Commas

☐ **Did you use a comma to separate the items listed in a row?**

EXAMPLE: *On my trip to the moon I took a spacesuit, crayons, a journal, and my cat.*

LOOK BACK

What parts of the story were easy or hard to picture in your mind? Write your answer below.

Think about Your Reading

READERS' CHECKLIST

Ease

☐ **Was the reading easy to read?**

☐ **Were you able to read it smoothly?**

5

Volcanoes

What do you know about volcanoes? What are they? What do they look like? What makes them explode?

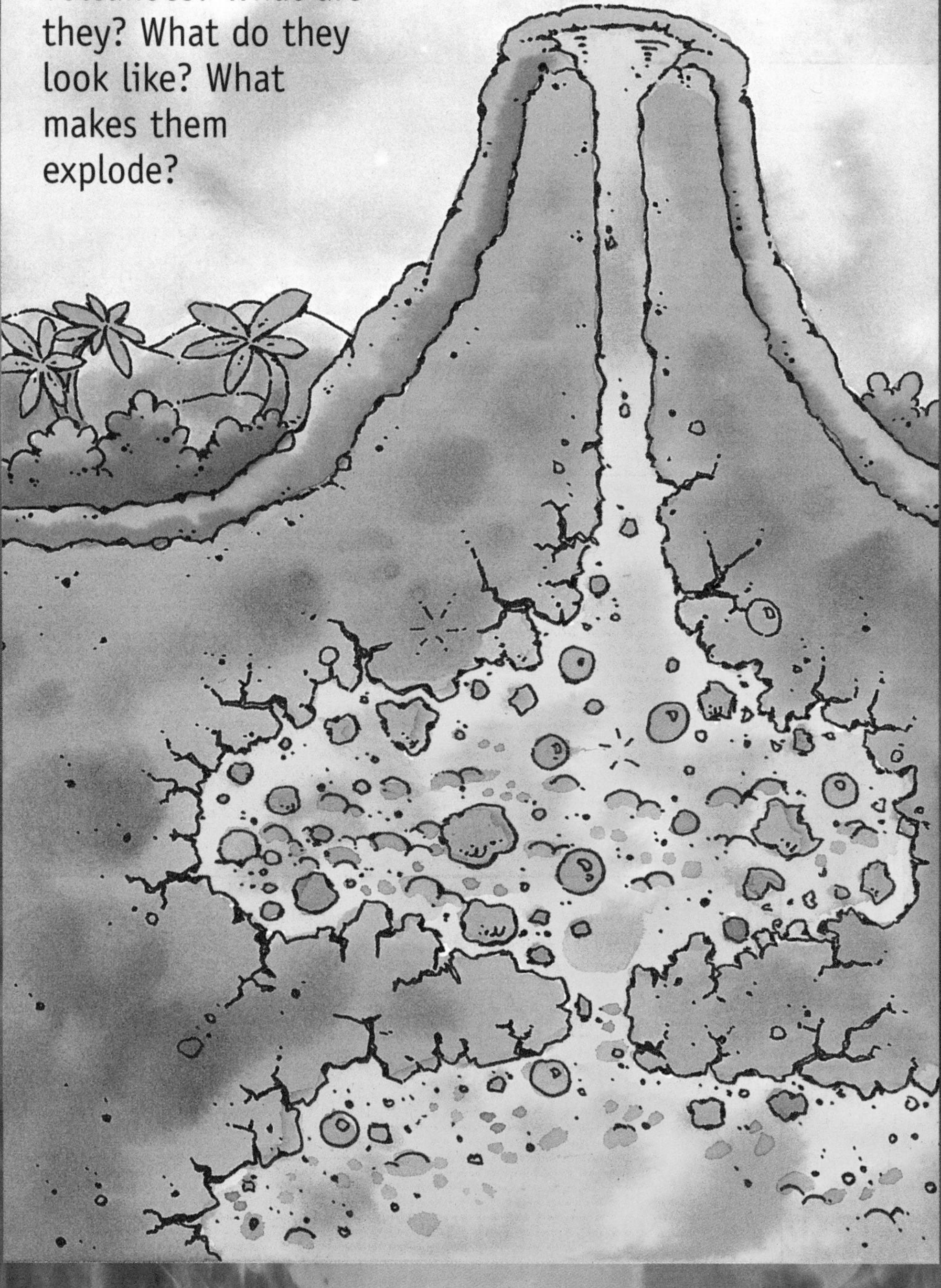

I. BEFORE YOU READ

Look over, or preview, this reading about volcanoes to get an idea of what you'll be learning about.

1. First, read the title.
2. Next, read the first and the last paragraphs.
3. Then, write 3 questions you have about volcanoes.

MY QUESTIONS

1.

2.

3.

MY PURPOSE

What is the main idea? What makes a volcano blow its top?

II. READ

Read this part of the book *Volcanoes.*

1. Underline parts of the text that tell why a volcano blows its top.
2. Read *Volcanoes* again. In the Notes, **make clear** information you learned by writing it down.

Volcanoes: Mountains That Blow Their Tops by Nicholas Nirgiotis

Response Notes

Long ago, people thought a god of fire lived inside volcanoes. They thought he liked to move from one volcano to another. Every time he moved he stirred things up. Today we know the facts. Volcanoes start deep in the earth.

EXAMPLE:

Volcanoes begin deep inside the earth.

The earth is round—like an orange. It is made of layers of rock. The top layer is called the crust. It is like the skin of the orange.

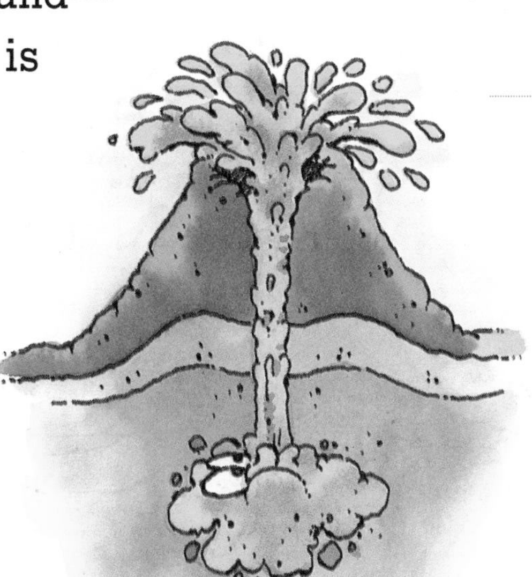

volcanoes (vol•**ca**•noes)—mountains that have a hole that can shoot out lava, ash, and gasses.
stirred—mixed.
layers (lay•ers)—different parts, one on top of the other.

The layer below is called the mantle. The mantle is very hot. So some of the rock melts. The melted rock is called magma.

STOP AND THINK **stop and think** STOP AND THINK

How is the earth like an orange?

STOP AND THINK STOP AND THINK STOP AND THINK

The magma is moving too. It pushes up on the plates. Sometimes the magma finds a crack between the plates. Then—SPURT! Out it comes. This is the start of a volcano.

plates—top layers of the earth. They move very slowly.

VOLCANOES (continued)

Response notes

The magma bubbles up a tube. The tube is like a long straw. At the top is a hole. The hole is called a crater. The magma spills out of the crater. Now the magma is called lava.

One kind of lava flows much more slowly.

flows—moves.

STOP AND THINK **stop and think** STOP AND THINK

How does a volcano start?

STOP AND THINK STOP AND THINK STOP AND THINK

Response Notes

Sometimes it sprays out of the crater into the sky. In the air the lava hardens into sharp rocks and ash. Then black clouds of ash fill the sky. They block out the sun, so it is dark—even at noon!

ash—powder left behind when something burns.

reread

Read *Volcanoes* again. Look for details that help you understand why a volcano blows its top. Be sure you answered the **Stop and Think** questions.

WORD WORK

Think about these 2 rules.

RULE #1: With words that end in **silent *e***, remember to drop the ***e*** before adding an ending that starts with a vowel. Example: make + ing = *making*

RULE # 2: With words that end in 2 consonants (*pack, yell*) or have 2 vowels that are side by side in the middle (*scoop, load*), you need to just add the endings to the word. Example: pack + ing = *packing*; scoop + ed = *scooped*

1. Read the words in the box below.
2. Write them under the correct heading in the chart.
3. Add *-ed* or *-ing* to each word.

WORD BOX

live	move	melt
like	seem	push

CHART

Silent *e* Words + *ing*	Other Words + *ed*
1.	1.
2.	2.
3.	3.

READING REMINDER

Look for the main idea when you read nonfiction.

GET READY TO WRITE

PLAN YOUR WRITING

Fill in 4 more details that help explain the main idea below. You'll use this page to plan a paragraph.

MAIN IDEA
Hot magma in the earth makes a volcano blow its top.

Detail 1

Magma moves and pushes up on the plates.

Detail 2

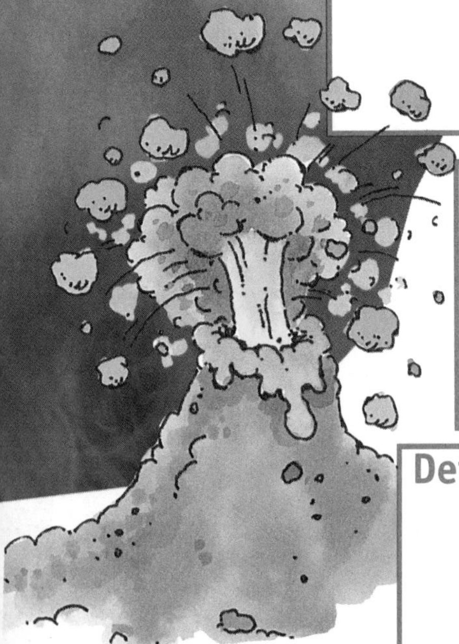

Detail 3

Detail 4

Detail 5

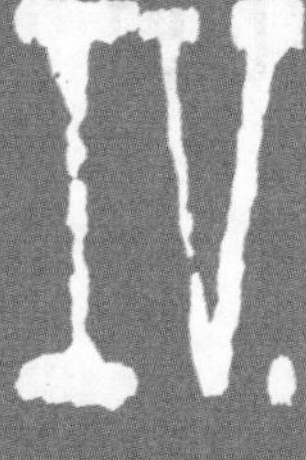

WRITE

Write a **paragraph** that explains how a volcano starts.

1. Use the 5 details to write the rest of your paragraph.
2. Wrap up with a closing sentence that gives a volcano another name. Example: *A volcano is an angry mountain.*
3. Give your paragraph a title.
4. Use the Writers' Checklist to edit your paragraph.

Title:

Hot magma in the earth makes a volcano blow its top.

Continue writing your paragraph on the next page.

Continue your paragraph below.

WRITERS' CHECKLIST

Capitalization

- ☐ **Does each sentence start with a capital letter?** EXAMPLE: *Magma moves upward.*
- ☐ **Did you use capital letters in the main words of the title?** EXAMPLE: *Mountains into Volcanoes*

V. LOOK BACK

What did you enjoy most as you read about volcanoes? Write your answer below.

Think about Your Reading

READERS' CHECKLIST

Enjoyment

- ☐ **Did you like the reading?**
- ☐ **Would you recommend the reading to a friend?**

Cave People

Take a trip into the past. Pretend you are living with cave people. How do you think your life would change?

I. BEFORE YOU READ

Fill in the K-W-L Chart below.

1. Write all you know about cave people under the **K**.

2. Write what you want to find out under the **W**. You will fill in the **L** part later.

3. Share what you know and what you want to learn with a partner.

K-W-L CHART

What I **K**now

What I **W**ant to Know

What I **L**earned

MY PURPOSE

What were cave people's lives like?

II. READ

Read this part of *Cave People*.

1. Circle important facts that **make clear** what cave people's lives were like.
2. Read *Cave People* again. In the Notes, jot down new facts that you learned.

Cave People by Linda Hayward

Response Notes

It is fifty thousand years ago. These hunters are hungry. They need meat.

They see a mammoth. But it is too big for them to hunt. The men hide until it goes away.

These hunters have spotted a reindeer! The hunters come closer.

The reindeer tries to fight back. But the hunters kill it with their spears.

EXAMPLE:

Cave people used spears to kill animals.

Who are these hunters? They are called Neanderthals. (You say it like this: nee-AN-der-thals.) These people lived in caves long, long ago.

It was the Ice Age—the time of the mammoth and the cave bear. Winters were long and dark.

mammoth (mam•moth)—very big, thick-haired elephant that used to live a long time ago.
spotted (spot•ted)—seen.
reindeer (rein•deer)—deer that lives in cold areas.
spears—weapons that are long sticks with pointed heads.

Response Notes

Even the summers were cold.

The Neanderthals had big teeth and low foreheads. They had bony ridges above their eyes. Their bodies were short and thick. The Neanderthals really did not look that different from people today. But they were probably much stronger. They had to be.

STOP AND THINK **stop and think** STOP AND THINK

How are Neanderthals like people today?

STOP AND THINK **stop and think** STOP AND THINK

Life was hard. Neanderthals spent much of their time finding food and just trying to stay alive.

A lion could spring out of nowhere! Neanderthals had to be ready for all kinds of dangers.

ridges (ridg•es)—deep lines.

reread

Read *Cave People* again. Think about what life was like for the Neanderthals. Go back to page 62 and fill out the **L** (What I **L**earned) section. Then, be sure you answered the **Stop and Think** question.

WORD WORK

Words have beats—1, 2, 3, or more beats. Try clapping *mammoth*. You clapped 2 times because *mam/moth* has 2 beats or **syllables** (sill-uh-bulls).

Some 2 syllable words have 2 consonant letters in the middle. These letters can be the same (*bot/tle*). These letters can be different (*bas/ket, win/dow*).

mammoth hunter reindeer winters
shorter summers better

1. Put words with the same consonants in the middle in the left-hand column.
2. Put words with 2 different consonants in the middle in the right-hand column.
3. Put a line between the consonants to divide each word.

Same Consonants	Different Consonants
mam/moth	hun/ter

READING REMINDER

Look for answers to the 5 W's when you read nonfiction: who?, what?, when?, where?, and why?

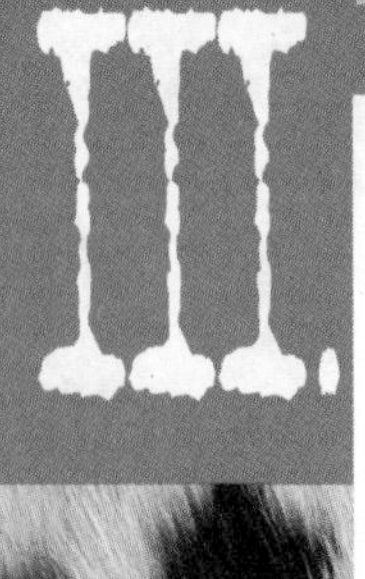

GET READY TO WRITE

PREWRITE

Pretend you are a news reporter and complete the chart below. You have to write a news story about cave people on a big hunt. All news stories have a headline and answer 5 questions: who, what, when, where, and why.

Headline:

Topic Sentence: Hunting for your dinner is not an easy thing to do.

Who:

What: They hunt for reindeer. Mammoths are too big.

When:

Where:

Why:

Closing:

IV. WRITE

Use your notes on page 66 to help you write a **news story**. Include a headline, an opening topic sentence, and a closing sentence.

1. Be sure to answer each question: who, what, where, when, and why.
2. Use the Writers' Checklist to edit your news story.

Headline:

Continue writing your news story on the next page.

Continue writing your news story.

WRITERS' CHECKLIST

End Punctuation

☐ **Did you use correct punctuation at the end of each sentence?**
EXAMPLE: *The cave people were always looking for food.* *When did the cave people hunt?*

V. LOOK BACK

What did you learn about cave people? Write what you learned below.

Think about Your Reading

READERS' CHECKLIST

Understanding

☐ **Did you understand the reading?**
☐ **Can you tell a friend what the reading is about?**

Look at Your Eyes

Have you ever wondered why you close your eyes when you go from the dark into the bright sunlight? What happens to your eyes when you go from dark to light?

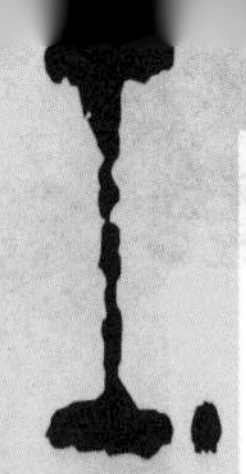

BEFORE YOU READ

Preview the reading *Look at Your Eyes*.

1. First, read the title.

2. Read the first and last paragraphs.

3. Then answer each previewing question below.

PREVIEWING QUESTIONS

1. What do you think *Look at Your Eyes* is about?

2. What do you know already about the word *pupil*?

3. What facts did you learn from previewing?

MY PURPOSE

What causes the pupil of an eye to change size?

READ

Read this part of the book *Look at Your Eyes*.

1. Underline any parts that make you ask questions about the changes in the eyes.
2. Write your **questions** in the Notes.

Look at Your Eyes
by Paul Showers

Did you ever watch the pupil in your eye change its size? This is how I do it.

I close my eyes almost all the way. I keep them open so I can see just a little. I count to ten.

One—two—three—four—up to ten. Then I open my eyes wide. I watch one pupil in the mirror. It grows smaller as soon as I open my eyes.

Response Notes

EXAMPLE:

How big is the pupil?

cause and effect

What is the effect (or result) of the cause below?

Cause:	Effect:
You close your eyes, then open them in bright light.	

pupil (pu•pil)—opening in the center of the eye in which light comes.

Response notes

Why does the pupil change its size? The pupil is a little round window. It lets the light into your eye.

When your eye needs a lot of light, the pupil gets big. When your eye only needs a little light, the pupil gets small.

Your pupil gets big when you are in a dark room, or when you are outdoors at night. Then your eye needs all the light it can get.

Your pupil grows big to let in every bit of light.

reread

Read *Look at Your Eyes* again and think about the changes in the eye. As you read again, be sure you answered the **Cause-Effect** question.

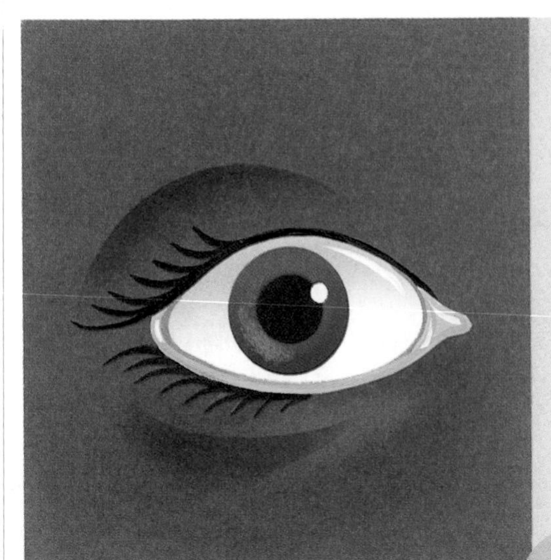

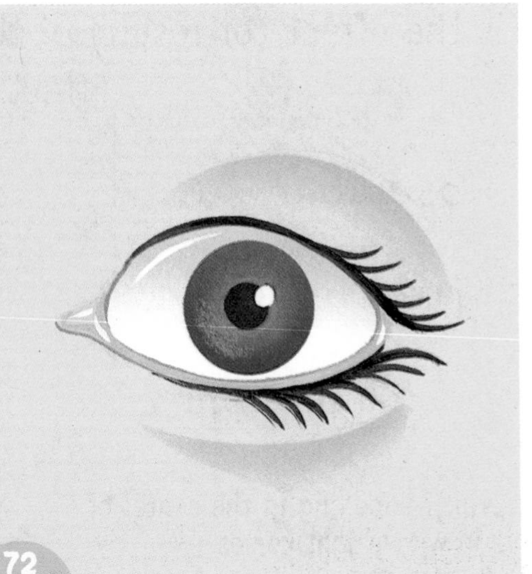

WORD WORK

Adding letters to the beginning and end of a word makes the word longer. It can also change the word's meaning. A **prefix** is a part of a word added to the beginning of a word. A **suffix** is a part of a word added to the end of a word.

Example: The smaller word is *mind*. Add the prefix *re-* and the suffix *-er*. The new word is *reminder*.

Build long words by adding beginnings and endings to the words below. One example has been done for you.

re + open *reopen*	dark + est
small + ish	wide + en
un + light + ed	grow + ing
look + ing	count + er

READING REMINDER

Asking questions about cause and effect helps you think about what you are reading.

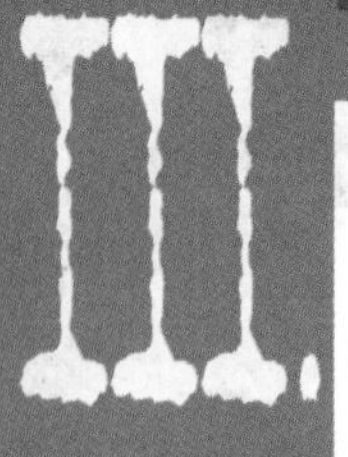

GET READY TO WRITE

WRITING ABOUT A TOPIC

Use the planner below to prepare to write a paragraph that explains why your eyes change.

TOPIC SENTENCE

What do you want to say about your eyes?

DETAIL SENTENCES

What causes your eyes to change?

What happens when your eyes change?

CLOSING SENTENCE

What do you think about how your eyes change?

Write a **paragraph** that explains why your eyes change.

1. Use your paragraph planner on page 74. Begin with the topic sentence, add 2 detail sentences, and end with a closing sentence.
2. Use the Writers' Checklist to edit your paragraph.

Title:

Continue writing your paragraph on the next page.

Continue your paragraph

WRITERS' CHECKLIST

Commas

☐ **Did you place a comma between two sentences that you joined with *and, but, or,* or *for*?** EXAMPLE: *Sometimes the pupils get larger, and sometimes they get smaller.*

V. LOOK BACK

What did you learn about your eyes from reading *Look at Your Eyes*? Write what you learned below.

Think about Your Reading

READERS' CHECKLIST

Meaning

☐ **Did you learn something from this reading?**

☐ **Did you have a strong feeling about one part of the reading?**

Just a Few Words, Mr. Lincoln

Do you ever wonder what it might be like to be the president? Read on to find out more about President Abraham Lincoln.

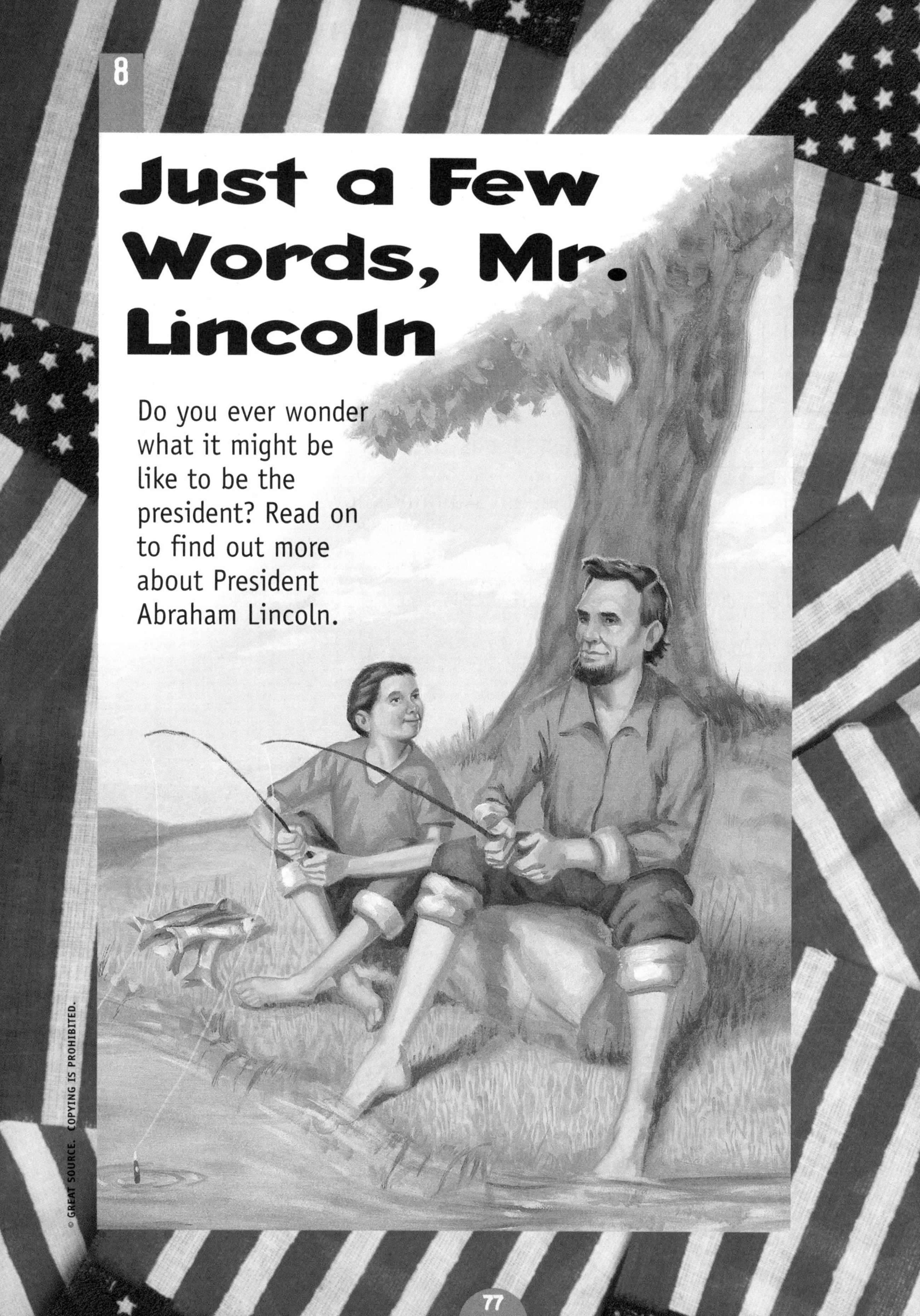

BEFORE YOU READ

Read the statements below.

1. If you agree, check the AGREE box. If you disagree, check the DISAGREE box.
2. Share your ideas with your reading partner.

AGREE	DISAGREE	
☐	☐	Presidents are not afraid of anything.
☐	☐	A great speech takes a long time to write.
☐	☐	The president is the leader of the country.
☐	☐	The president's family knows he is often busy.

What do you think *Just a Few Words, Mr. Lincoln* will be about?

....

....

....

....

....

MY PURPOSE

How is the story of Lincoln like experiences I've had?

READ

Read this part of *Just a Few Words, Mr. Lincoln*.

1. Read it once and underline parts that are in some way like your own life.
2. Read it again and write in the Notes how parts of the story **connect** to experiences you've had.

Just a Few Words, Mr. Lincoln
by Jean Fritz

Response Notes

EXAMPLE:

When I was very sick last year, I went to a lot of doctors.

Tad wasn't around while his father was writing. He was in bed. Sick. The doctor didn't know what was wrong. That was not a good sign, Mrs. Lincoln said. She was beside herself with worry. The president was too. He just hoped Tad could be better before he went to Gettysburg.

On November 18, Lincoln had to leave. And Tad was not better. His fever was still high. Of course Tad had to take medicine, but he didn't like it. Sometimes only

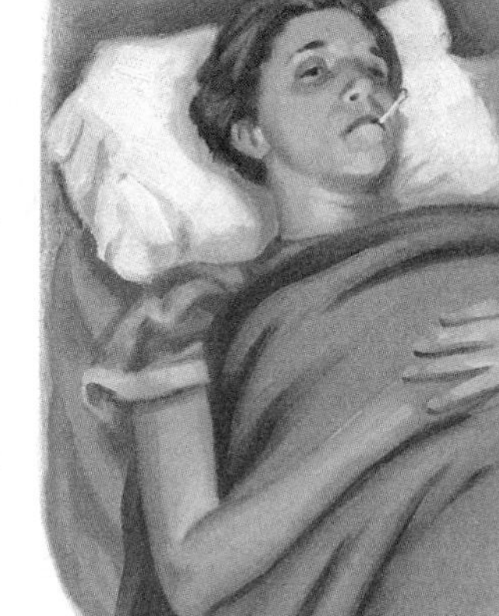

sign—hint of something to come.

Gettysburg (Get•tys•burg)—place in the state of Pennsylvania where an important battle of the Civil War was fought.

Response Notes

his father could get him to take it. And his father was leaving. It was hard for Lincoln to say good-bye. But he had to.

STOP AND THINK **stop and think** STOP AND THINK

Why did Lincoln not want to leave?

STOP AND THINK STOP AND THINK STOP AND THINK

Lincoln went to Gettysburg in a special four-car train. It was <u>decorated</u> with red, white, and blue <u>streamers</u>. And it was filled with important people. All of them wanted to talk with the president.

So the president talked. All the way to Gettysburg. The story is told that

decorated (dec•o•rat•ed)—dressed up; made pretty.

streamers (stream•ers)—thin strips of paper used to make something look nice and special.

Response Notes

JUST A FEW WORDS, MR. LINCOLN (continued)

Lincoln wrote his speech on the train. Just scratched it out on the back of an old envelope. That is not true. His speech was in his pocket—all written except for a last "lick."

STOP AND THINK **stop and think** STOP AND THINK

What happened on the train?

STOP AND THINK STOP AND THINK STOP AND THINK

In Gettysburg everyone wanted to honor the president. That evening a group of singers sang to him and then asked for a speech. But the president told them he had nothing to say. If he tried, he might say something

scratched—quickly wrote.
"lick"—little bit.
honor (hon•or)—show special respect.
evening (eve•ning)—night.

STOP AND THINK **stop and think** STOP AND THINK

What happened when the singers asked Lincoln to give them a speech?

STOP AND THINK STOP AND THINK STOP AND THINK

Response Notes

JUST A FEW WORDS, MR. LINCOLN (continued)

foolish. The singers didn't think much of that. They just hoped the president would do better the next day.

Gettysburg was crowded with visitors. Important visitors. In the house where Lincoln was staying, there were not even enough beds to go around. Mr. Everett was told

foolish (fool•ish)—silly.
crowded (crowd•ed)—full of many people.
visitors (vis•i•tors)—people who stay for a short time.

Response Notes

JUST A FEW WORDS, MR. LINCOLN (continued)

he might have to share his bed with the governor. But at the last minute another bed was found for the governor.

Mr. Everett's daughter was not so lucky. She had to share her bed with two other ladies. It was too much for the bed. It broke down in the middle of the night. The three ladies crashed to the floor.

President Lincoln, of course, had a room to himself. But before going to bed, he went over his speech. He gave it a last lick. Yet he kept thinking about Tad. How was he? Had

governor (gov•er•nor)—person who is in charge of a state.
crashed—fell.

STOP AND THINK **stop and think** STOP AND THINK

How do you know Abraham Lincoln really loved his son, Tad?

STOP AND THINK STOP AND THINK STOP AND THINK

Response Notes

Just a Few Words, Mr. Lincoln (continued)

the fever gone down? Luckily, a telegram arrived from Mrs. Lincoln. Tad was much better, she said. That was just what Lincoln wanted to hear. He had never read sweeter-sounding words.

telegram (tel•e•gram)— message.

reread

Reread *Just a Few Words, Mr. Lincoln*. As you do, think about how your experiences connect to what happened in the story. Be sure to answer all the **Stop and Think** questions.

WORD WORK

Take a prefix off the beginning of a word and a suffix off the end. The small word that's left is called a **base word**.

Look at the words below.

1. If there's a prefix (*re-* or *un-*), put a line through it.
2. If there's a suffix (*-ed, -ing*), put a line through it.
3. Now write the small word that's called the base word. One has been done for you.

Long Word	Base Word
a. filled	fill
b. sounding	
c. talked	
d. singers	
e. crowded	
f. redo	
g. rethink	
h. unable	

READING REMINDER

When you make personal connections to a story, you will remember it better.

GET READY TO WRITE

PREWRITE

Lincoln didn't want to say good-bye to his family. When have you felt this way?

1. Think of a time in your life when you did not want to leave home.
2. Make notes in the boxes below.

Why didn't I want to leave home?

Who was with me?

What did I feel?

When did this happen?

What did others say and do?

How did I feel later?

IV. WRITE

Write a **journal entry** about a time you didn't want to leave home.

1. Use the notes on page 86 for ideas.

2. In the closing sentence, tell how you felt.

3. Use the Writers' Checklist to help you edit.

Continue writing your journal entry on the next page.

Continue your journal entry.

WRITERS' CHECKLIST

Capitalization

☐ **Did you put commas between the names of a city and a state?** EXAMPLE: *Chicago, Illinois; Nashville, Tennessee*

LOOK BACK

What would you tell a friend *Just a Few Words, Mr. Lincoln* is about? Write your answer below.

Think about Your Reading

READERS' CHECKLIST

Understanding

☐ **What was the reading about?**

☐ **What would you tell a friend about the reading?**

9

Why I Sneeze, Shiver, Hiccup, and Yawn

Have you ever just started to hiccup? Have you ever tried to stop sneezing? Why do people do these funny things?

BEFORE YOU READ

Fill in the K-W-L Chart below.

1. Write all you know about why people sneeze, shiver, hiccup, and yawn under the **K**.
2. Write what you want to find out under the **W**. You will fill in the **L** part after you read.
3. Share what you know and want to learn with a partner.

K-W-L CHART

What I **K**now

What I **W**ant to Know

What I **L**earned

MY PURPOSE

Why do people sneeze, shiver, hiccup, and yawn?

II. READ

Read this part of *Why I Sneeze, Shiver, Hiccup, and Yawn*.

1. As you read it the first time, highlight details that explain what makes people sneeze, shiver, hiccup, and yawn.
2. Then read it again. This time write notes that **make clear** what you learned.

Why I Sneeze, Shiver, Hiccup, and Yawn by Melvin Berger

You are playing hide-and-seek. You've found a good hiding place. You want to be as quiet as you can. All of a sudden—KA-CHOO! You sneeze. Everyone knows where you are.

Why do you sneeze—even when you don't want to?

You are eating lunch with your friends. You are in the middle of telling them a story. All at once you hiccup. HIC! Your friends start to laugh. HIC! You try to stop. HIC! But you can't. HIC!

Why do you hiccup—even when you don't want to?

A sneeze is a reflex. So is a hiccup. You don't have to think about making reflexes happen.

Response Notes

EXAMPLE:

A sneeze is a reflex you can't control.

Response Notes

They happen whether you want them to or not. They happen very fast, and it is hard to stop them. Shivering and yawning are also reflexes. All reflexes work through your nervous system.

STOP AND THINK **stop and think** STOP AND THINK

What would you tell a friend about sneezes?

Your nervous system is made up of two parts. One part is the nerves. The nerves look like long, thin threads. They reach all over your body.

The other part is the spinal cord and brain. The spinal cord is a thick bundle of nerves. It is inside your spine, or

Response Notes

backbone. The brain is at the upper end of the spinal cord. It is made up of billions of tiny nerves.

Nerves are like telephone wires. They carry messages back and forth. The brain and spinal cord are like the main office of the telephone company. All the messages must go through here.

STOP AND THINK **stop and think** STOP AND THINK

What have you learned about nerves?

STOP AND THINK STOP AND THINK STOP AND THINK

Suppose you put your finger on a hot stove. The nerves in your hand <u>sense</u> that the stove is hot. They send out a message.

sense—feel.

Response Notes

The message speeds along nerves from your hand to your spinal cord. Here the message passes to a different nerve. This nerve controls the muscles that move your arm.

A signal flashes through the nerve. It tells your muscles to move your hand—and fast. Before you even know what hurts, your hand jerks away from the stove.

signal (sig•nal)—message.
flashes (flash•es)—goes quickly.
jerks—quickly moves away.

STOP AND THINK stop and think STOP AND THINK

What do nerves do?

WHY I SNEEZE (continued)

Response Notes

Pulling your hand off a hot stove is a reflex. It happens very quickly, and it is not completely under your control. It happens automatically, without your having to think about making it happen.

completely (com•**plete**•ly)—all.
automatically (au•to•**mat**•i•cal•ly)—naturally, without thought.

STOP AND THINK stop and think STOP AND THINK

What is one important fact you learned about why people sneeze, shiver, yawn, and hiccup?

reread

Reread *Why I Sneeze* again. Be sure you have answered all the **Stop and Think** questions. Then take time to fill in what you learned under the **L** part of the K-W-L chart on page 90.

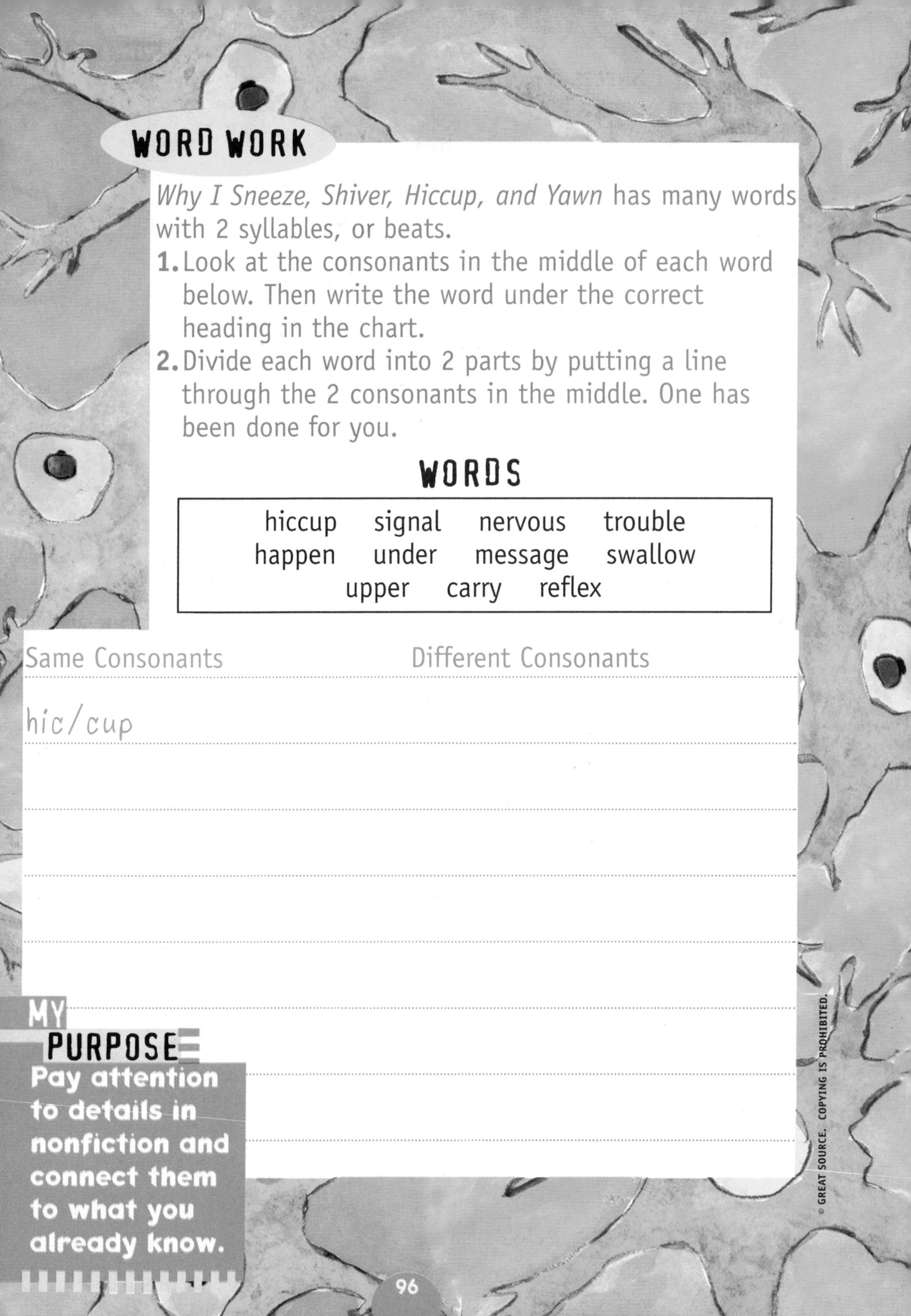

WORD WORK

Why I Sneeze, Shiver, Hiccup, and Yawn has many words with 2 syllables, or beats.

1. Look at the consonants in the middle of each word below. Then write the word under the correct heading in the chart.
2. Divide each word into 2 parts by putting a line through the 2 consonants in the middle. One has been done for you.

WORDS

hiccup signal nervous trouble
happen under message swallow
upper carry reflex

Same Consonants	Different Consonants
hic/cup	

MY PURPOSE

Pay attention to details in nonfiction and connect them to what you already know.

III. GET READY TO WRITE

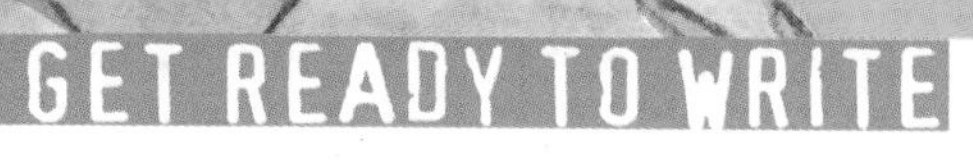

A. FIND DETAILS

Get ready to write a paragraph about this reading. The main idea is what a selection is mostly about. A good writer supports the main idea with details.

1. Look back at your Notes and what you highlighted.
2. Find 4 details that support the main idea. Write them below.

THE MAIN IDEA

I sneeze, shiver, hiccup, and yawn because they are reflexes.

DETAIL

DETAIL

DETAIL

DETAIL

B. WRITE A CLOSING SENTENCE

A paragraph should end with a closing sentence that wraps up and restates the main idea.

1. Write 2 different closing sentences that explain what you think about reflexes.

CLOSING SENTENCE 1

CLOSING SENTENCE 2

2. Decide which of the 2 sentences will make a better closing sentence for your paragraph. Put a star (☆) by it.

IV. WRITE

Write a **paragraph** explaining why you sneeze, shiver, hiccup, and yawn.

1. Begin by writing your topic sentence below. It is the main idea.
2. Choose 3 details to support your topic sentence.
3. Start a new sentence for each detail and end with your closing sentence.
4. Use the Writers' Checklist to edit your paragraph.

Title:

Continue writing your paragraph on the next page.

Continue your paragraph below.

WRITERS' CHECKLIST

Capitalization

- ☐ **Did you capitalize the first word in each sentence?**
  EXAMPLE: ***A** sneeze is a reflex.*
- ☐ **Did you capitalize the word *I*?**
  EXAMPLE: *A reflex is something **I** can't control.*

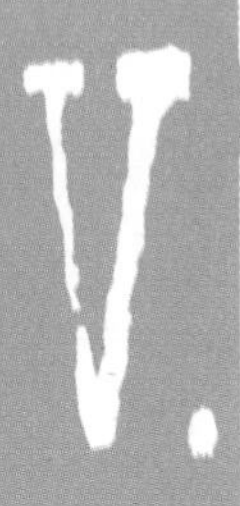

V. LOOK BACK

What parts of the reading did you like? What parts didn't you like? Write your answer below.

Think about Your Reading — READERS' CHECKLIST

Enjoyment

- ☐ **Did you like the reading?**
- ☐ **Would you recommend the reading to a friend?**

Marvin Redpost: Alone in His Teacher's House

Sometimes taking care of a pet can be hard. Think of all of the things that might go wrong. Marvin Redpost has lots to do when he takes care of his teacher's dog because things do go wrong!

I. BEFORE YOU READ

With a reading partner, take turns reading the questions below.

1. Think about each question. Trade ideas with your partner.
2. Write your answers below.

1. Why might a pet not want to eat?

2. What things could you do if you could not get your pet to eat?

3. Who could help you solve the problem?

MY PURPOSE

What is Marvin like?

READ

Read this part of a story about a boy named Marvin Redpost.

1. First, read and underline parts of the story that show what Marvin is like.
2. Then read the story again. This time write in the Notes how what Marvin does **connects** to things that you do.

Marvin Redpost: Alone in His Teacher's House by Louis Sachar

He filled the bowl with fresh dog food.

"Here you go," he said, setting it down in front of the old whisker-faced dog.

Waldo didn't even look at it.

Marvin picked out a piece of dog food and held it in front of Waldo's nose. "Yum, yum," he said.

Waldo turned his head away. He whined.

Marvin sat on the kitchen floor and stroked his back. "I tell you what," he said. "If I eat it, will you?"

Response Notes

EXAMPLE:

I have to feed our dog, too.

whined—made a crying sound.
stroked—pet.

Response Notes

The bit of dog food was still in his hand.

Marvin opened his mouth wide so Waldo could see. He took the bit of dog food between his thumb and forefinger and held it inside his mouth.

He was careful not to let it touch his tongue.

He quickly pulled out his hand, closed his mouth, and swallowed.

"Yum, delicious!" he said.

The dog food was hidden in his fist.

Waldo wasn't fooled.

"Okay," said Marvin. "I'll really eat it this time. But then you have to, too."

Waldo watched him.

Marvin touched the dog food with his tongue. It wasn't

forefinger (fore•fin•ger)—first finger after the thumb.
delicious (de•li•cious)—tastes good.
fooled—tricked.

MARVIN REDPOST (continued)

Response Notes

horrible. It tasted a little like cereal.

He bit into it.

It was chewier than cereal. And a little bit gritty, like it had tiny seeds in it.

DOUBLE-ENTRY JOURNAL

Quote	What This Tells You About Marvin
"Marvin touched the dog food with his tongue."	

He chewed and swallowed.

It wasn't gross. It wasn't something he'd ask his mom to get for an after-school snack. But it really wasn't too bad.

"Okay, your turn," he said. Waldo whined. "Like this," said Marvin. He crawled to Waldo's bowl and picked out a piece of

horrible (hor•ri•ble)—very bad.
chewier (chew•i•er)—harder to mash with teeth.
gritty (grit•ty)—full of rough bits.

Response Notes

dog food with his teeth.

He chewed it up and swallowed. He smiled at Waldo. "Delicious!" he said.

Waldo lay his whiskered face against the floor.

Waldo pushed his head under Marvin's hand.

Marvin petted him. "Nick and Stuart hate me," he said. "They say I think I'm better than everyone. I don't think I'm better than everyone. I just have a job to do."

DOUBLE-ENTRY JOURNAL

Quote	What This Tells You About Marvin
"I don't think I'm better than everyone. I just have a job to do."	

Response Notes

Waldo licked Marvin across the face with his big tongue.

Marvin petted him some more, then stood up. He checked to make sure the key was in his pocket. "I'll be back after dinner," he promised. "*With liver!*"

He tried his best to sound enthusiastic.

His mother said she'd take him to the store after dinner to buy the liver. And then drive him to Mrs. North's house.

"Can I come?" asked Jacob. "I've never seen the inside of a real teacher's house."

"Sure," said Marvin, glad to impress his older brother.

"Me too," said Linzy, "I want to meet Waldo."

liver **(liv•er)**—body part of animals and humans, found near the stomach. Some people eat animal liver as food.

enthusiastic (en•thu•si•as•tic)—full of interest and energy.

impress (im•press)—make someone else think you have done something good.

Response Notes

Marvin's father went along too. "I don't want to be a party pooper," he said.

Marvin smiled. After all his troubles, it felt good to have his family with him.

He paid for the liver out of his own money. A quarter pound only cost 37¢. Less than a candy bar.

Inside Mrs. North's house, Marvin found a pot and filled it with water. He turned on the stove. His mother offered to cook the liver for him, but Marvin said, "No, it's part of my job."

He dropped the slimy meat into the boiling water.

Jacob was walking around the house. "Cool," he said as he went from one room to another.

party pooper (par•ty poop•er)—person who ruins the fun for everyone else.
quarter (quar•ter)—one of four equal parts; 1/4.
offered (of•fered)—volunteered.
boiling (boil•ing)—very hot; 212°.

MARVIN REDPOST (continued)

Response Notes

Linzy hugged and petted and rolled around on the floor with Waldo. "I wuv you, Waldo," she said.

The liver was stinking up the kitchen.

Marvin let it boil for ten minutes, like Dr. Charles said. Then he plucked it out of the water with a fork and cut it up into bite-size pieces.

He really didn't think it would work. He had tasted liver. And he had tasted dog food.

He liked dog food better.

He put the liver on a regular plate and set it on the floor.

His family gathered around to watch.

"Look, Waldo, *liver!*" said Marvin.

Waldo didn't move.

"*Please*, Waldo, begged Linzy. She pushed the plate to him.

Waldo sniffed at it.

plucked—pulled out.
gathered (gath•ered)—came together.

Response Notes

Then he stood up, stuck his head over the plate, and ate a piece of liver.

Marvin and his family cheered.

Waldo ate another piece, then another. He didn't stop until the plate was empty.

Then he waddled over to his dog food bowl and ate all his dog food too.

"All he needed was an appetizer," said Marvin's mother.

Marvin was so happy he almost cried.

He washed and dried the pot, knife, fork, and plate.

cheered—shouted in happiness.
waddled (wad•dled)—took short steps and swayed, like a duck.
appetizer (ap•pe•tiz•er)—food eaten before the main meal.

reread

Read the story again. Look for things that Marvin does, says, or thinks. Be sure you have filled in the **Double-entry Journals**.

WORD WORK

Many of the words you know end in a final **silent *e***. Here are some: *taste*, *bake*, and *come*.

Words that end in **silent *e*** are tricky if you are adding an ending that begins with a vowel such as *-ed*, *-ing*, and *-er*. It's easy when you follow this rule:

If a word ends in a **silent *e***, drop the **e** before adding an ending that starts with a vowel.

Add *-ed* and *-ing* to the words in the chart that end in **silent *e***. One has been done for you.

Word	+ed	+ing
1. whine	whined	whining
2. promise		
3. stroke (to pet)		
4. rinse		
5. taste		
6. smile		

READING REMINDER

When you connect with what characters say, do, and feel, you can understand them and their problems.

III. GET READY TO WRITE

THINK ABOUT A CHARACTER

Get ready to write a journal entry that describes Marvin. A writer needs to back up a description with proof. Look at what a character does, says, or feels. Study the example and fill in the rest.

DESCRIPTION *responsible*

PROOF *Marvin buys and cooks the liver himself.*

DESCRIPTION *patient*

PROOF

Marvin

DESCRIPTION *caring*

PROOF

DESCRIPTION *funny*

PROOF

IV. WRITE

Use your notes on page 112 to write a **journal entry** that describes 3 things about Marvin.

1. Give proof from the story for each word you use to describe him.
2. Finish with a closing sentence that says how you feel.
3. Use the Writers' Checklist to help you edit.

Continue your journal entry on the next page.

Continue your journal entry below.

WRITERS' CHECKLIST

Apostrophes

☐ **Did you use apostrophes correctly in your contractions?**

EXAMPLES:

is + not = isn't

he + is = he's

do + not = don't

V. LOOK BACK

What would you tell someone about Marvin Redpost? Write your answer below.

Think about Your Reading

READERS' CHECKLIST

Understanding

☐ **Did you understand the reading?**

☐ **Can you tell a friend what the reading is about?**

11

Hungry, Hungry Sharks

What if you were a hungry shark? You might spot some blood and swim to it. Or you might swim to the body of a great white whale. What would happen next?

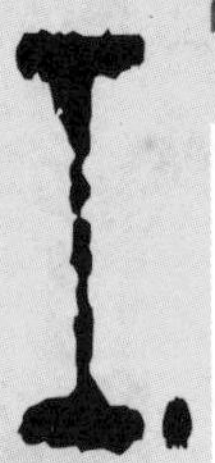

BEFORE YOU READ

Look over *Hungry, Hungry Sharks* before you read. When you preview, you look at and think about parts of a reading before you begin to read.

1. Read the title and the first and last paragraphs. Circle the most important words.
2. Answer the questions below.

WHAT WILL THIS READING BE ABOUT?

WHERE DOES *HUNGRY, HUNGRY SHARKS* TAKE PLACE?

WHAT DID YOU LEARN BY PREVIEWING *HUNGRY, HUNGRY SHARKS*?

MY PURPOSE

What are 3 details about sharks?

II. READ

Now read this part of the book *Hungry, Hungry Sharks*.

1. Read it once and underline at least 3 details that **make clear** what sharks are like.
2. Read it again and write any facts that surprise you in the Notes.

Hungry, Hungry Sharks
by Joanna Cole

These are blue sharks. They are far out at sea hunting for food. Suddenly they pick up the smell of blood.

The sharks speed up. They shoot through the water like torpedoes. In a few minutes they find a dead whale.

The blue sharks tear off big chunks of whale meat. Now the water is full of biting sharks.

shoot—move quickly.
torpedoes (**tor•pe•does**)—weapons that move underwater and explode.
chunks—large or thick parts.

Response Notes

EXAMPLE:

I didn't know that sharks could smell blood.

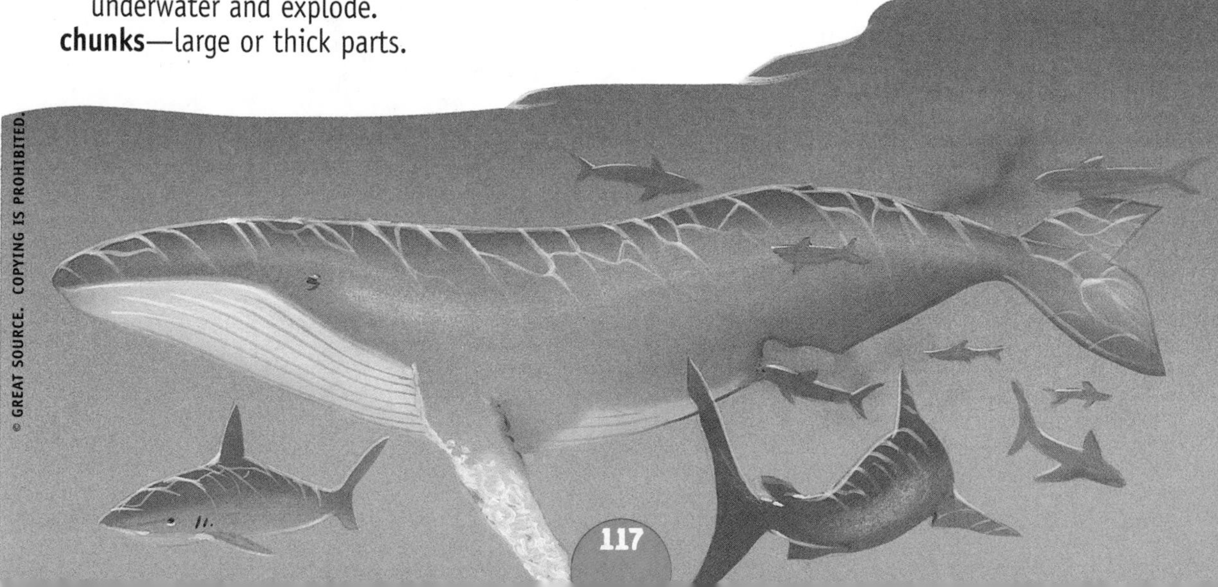

STOP AND THINK **stop and think** STOP AND THINK

How do blue sharks eat?

STOP AND THINK STOP AND THINK STOP AND THINK

Response Notes

Hungry, Hungry Sharks (continued)

If one shark gets hurt, the others turn on it. They will eat that shark too. In a short time the whale is all gone. The sharks swim away. Nothing is left. Nothing but bones.

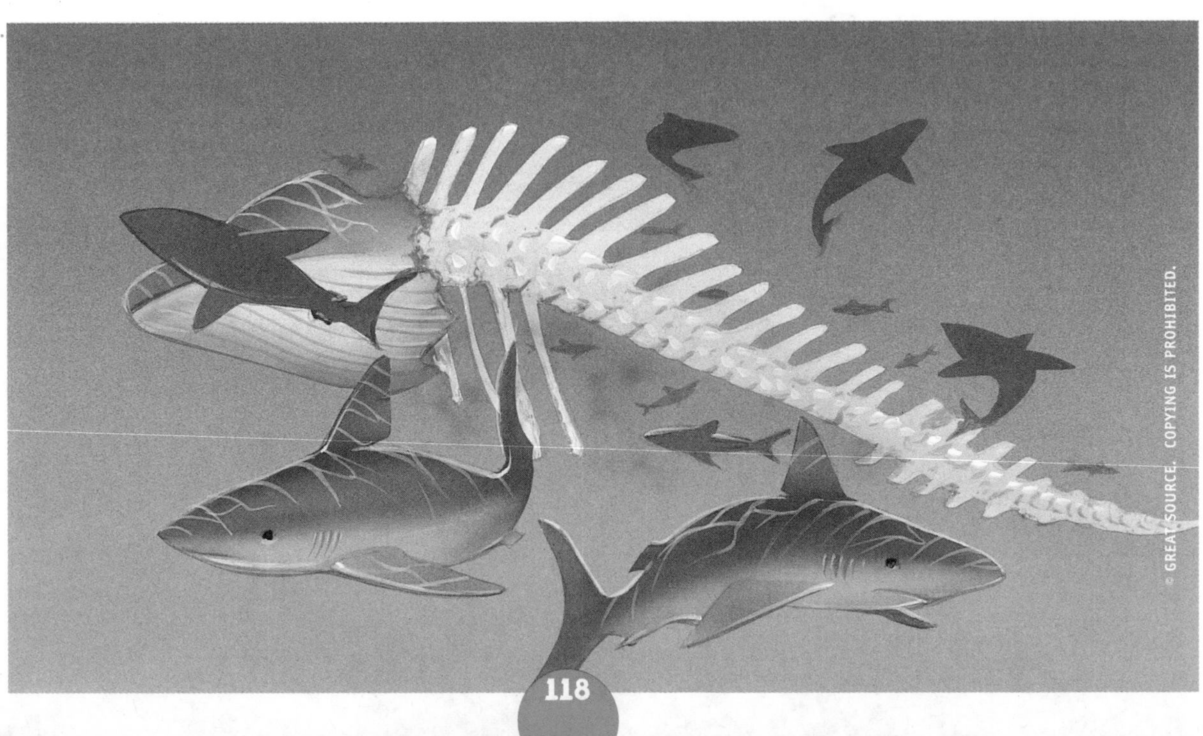

Hungry, Hungry Sharks (continued)

Response Notes

Blue sharks are called the wolves of the sea. This is because they stay together in packs. Blue sharks often swim after a ship for days. A long time ago sailors thought this meant that someone was going to die.

Why do blue sharks *really* follow ships? The sharks come because of noises from the ship. Then they stay to eat garbage that is thrown into the water.

STOP AND THINK **stop and think** STOP AND THINK

Why do blue sharks follow ships?

reread

Reread *Hungry, Hungry Sharks.* Think about the details you marked. Be sure to answer all the **Stop and Think** questions.

WORD WORK

If you can read one word, you can read a word that's like it or almost the same.

Example: You can read *pick*. Now take off the *p* and put *st* in front of *ick*. The new word is *stick*.

1. Make 2 new words for each word in the chart.
2. Change the beginning consonant or consonant cluster. One has been done for you.

EXAMPLES: fight	stick
sight	pick
speed	blow
1. bleed	
2.	
stay	call
1.	
2.	

READING REMINDER

The facts in nonfiction books help you learn about things you might never see.

GET READY TO WRITE

PREWRITE

Plan a paragraph that describes how sharks eat and act. Write notes under each heading in the web below. One has been done for you.

How blue sharks swim

How blue sharks eat

What sharks are called

blue sharks

How blue sharks know food is near

They smell blood.

What I think about sharks

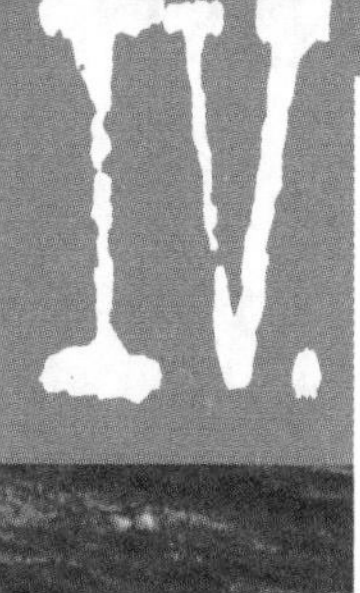

WRITE

Write a **paragraph** that describes blue sharks.

1. Number the ideas in the web you made on page 122. That is the order in which you write your ideas.
2. Complete the topic sentence below and use it to begin your paragraph.
3. End with a closing sentence that tells how you feel about blue sharks.
4. Use the Writers' Checklist to edit your paragraph.

Title: ______________________________

Topic Sentence: If you meet a blue shark in the ocean, ______________________________.

____

____

____

____

____

____

____

____

____

Continue writing your paragraph on the next page.

Continue writing your paragraph below.

WRITERS' CHECKLIST

Spelling

☐ Did you check your spelling? Ask a partner to help you check your work.

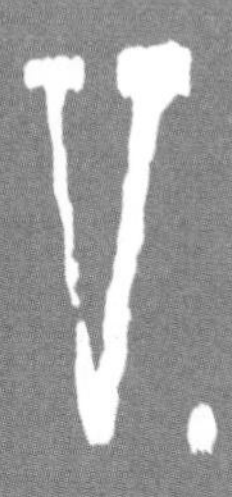

V. LOOK BACK

What 3 things did you learn about blue sharks? Write your answer below.

Think about Your Reading

READERS' CHECKLIST

Meaning

☐ Did you learn something from the reading?

☐ Did you have a strong feeling about one part of the reading?

12

Buffalo Bill and the Pony Express

Who was Buffalo Bill? What was the Pony Express? Read on to find out about what Buffalo Bill was like when he was young.

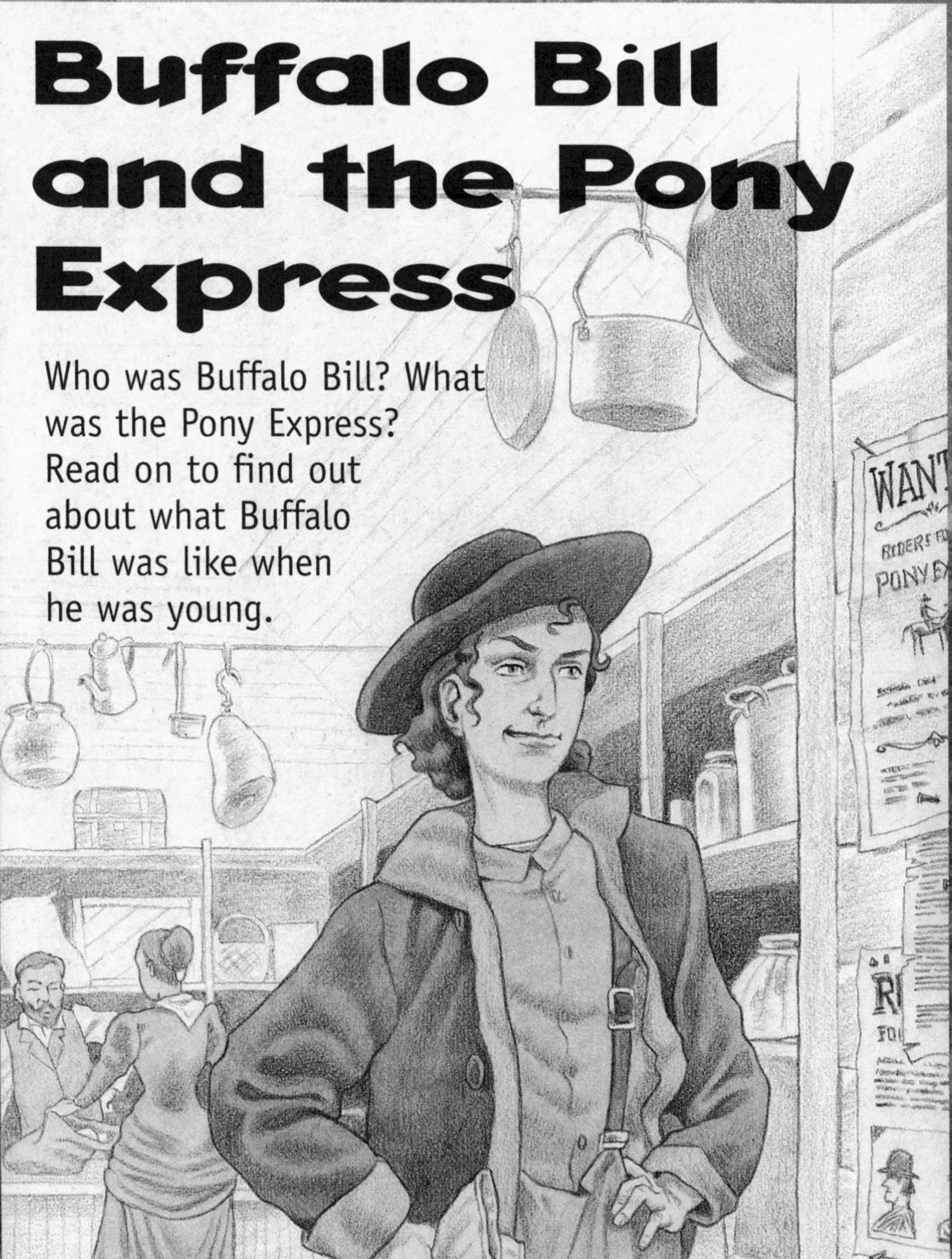

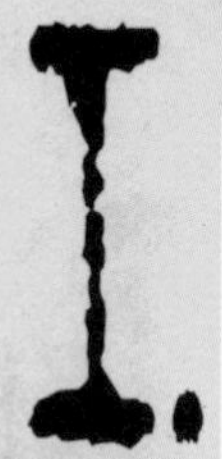

BEFORE YOU READ

Read the sentences below.

1. In the BEFORE column, check the items you agree with.
2. Share your feelings with a reading partner.

BEFORE agree	BEFORE disagree		AFTER agree	AFTER disagree
☐	☐	The Pony Express was a way of carrying the mail.	☐	☐
☐	☐	One Pony Express rider might go all day and all night.	☐	☐
☐	☐	Buffalo Bill knew how to swim, shoot, and ride.	☐	☐
☐	☐	Buffalo Bill didn't want to be a Pony Express rider.	☐	☐
☐	☐	Pony Express riders never ate or changed ponies while riding.	☐	☐

Write 1 question that you have about *Buffalo Bill and the Pony Express* before you read.

MY PURPOSE

What kind of person is Buffalo Bill, and how did he get to be a rider

READ

Read this part *of Buffalo Bill and the Pony Express*.

1. As you read the first time, underline parts that tell about what Buffalo Bill is like.
2. On your second reading, write any **questions** you have about Buffalo Bill in the Notes.

Buffalo Bill and the Pony Express by Eleanor Coerr

Response Notes

It was spring, 1860. Bill saw a sign in the post office at Fort Laramie. The sign said:

WANTED:

RIDERS FOR THE PONY EXPRESS

Young, skinny fellows under 18. Orphans welcome. $25 a week.

"That's the kind of job I want!" said Bill.

EXAMPLE: Does Buffalo Bill care about making a lot of money?

STORY FRAME

Setting

Where does the story take place?	When does the story take place?

Bill went in to see Mr. Majors. Bill stood tall and said, "I want to join the Pony Express."

fellows (**fel**•lows)—boys.
Orphans (**or**•phans)—children whose parents have died.

Response Notes

Mr. Majors laughed. "A big wind could blow you away!" he said. "You are too young."

"Gee whiz!" said Bill. "I'm sixteen!"

"Don't try to fool me!" said Mr. Majors. "If you are sixteen, then I'm a lizard."

STORY FRAME

What is Buffalo Bill's problem?

"I guess I'm closer to fifteen," said Bill.

"Can you ride? Follow trails? Swim? Shoot?" asked Mr. Majors.

"Yes, sir," said Bill. "I roped cattle when I was nine, and I can ride like the wind."

"It will be no picnic," said Mr. Majors. "You must ride

lizard (liz•ard)—reptile with scales and a long tail.
roped cattle (roped cat•tle)—caught cows, bulls, and oxen with long ropes called lassoes.
"It will be no picnic"—It will not be easy.

BUFFALO BILL (continued)

Response Notes

seventy or more miles each day. There may be trouble, too."

"I'm not afraid," Bill said.

"I like your spunk, son," said

STORY FRAME

Why is riding the Pony Express hard work?

Reason #1	Reason #2

Mr. Majors, "but you must promise not to lie, not to swear, and not to fight. And you must deliver the mail on time, no matter what."

"I promise," said Bill.

Mr. Majors showed Bill a map. "There's St. Joseph, and there's Sacramento, California. Eighty riders and four hundred ponies carry the mail between these cities," said Mr. Majors.

spunk—spirit; courage.
swear—say bad words.

Response Notes

"That's a long way!" said Bill.

"Yup," said Mr. Majors. "It's about two thousand miles. The riders travel all day and all night and carry the mail in ten days. They are twice as fast as stagecoaches."

Mr. Majors marked Red Buttes. "That is your home station," he said. "Your job is to take the mail from Red Buttes to Three Crossings."

"More than seventy-five miles on one pony?" asked Bill.

"Of course not!" said Mr. Majors. "Along the way there are stations with food, shelter, and fresh ponies. After two days' rest, you ride back with more letters."

stagecoaches (stage•coach•es**)**—carriages with four wheels that are pulled by horses.
station (sta•tion**)**—post; place.

reread

Read the story again. Think about what Buffalo Bill is like and be sure to fill in all of the **Story Frame** boxes. Go back also to page 126 and answer the questions again.

WORD WORK

Look at the example and words below.

1. Say the word.
2. Take off the ending (suffix).
3. Write the base word.
4. Make sure you add a final **silent *e*** to the base word if it's needed.

Word from Story	Base Word
a. rider	ride
b. closer	
c. roped	
d. promising	
e. riding	
f. chasing	
g. taking	
h. showed	

READING REMINDER

With nonfiction, read to answer the questions you have in your mind.

GET READY TO WRITE

PREWRITE

Get ready to write a letter describing Buffalo Bill and why he would make a good Pony Express rider. Answer the questions on the web about Buffalo Bill.

HOW WAS HE DARING?

proof from story

Bill asked to be part of the Pony Express even though he was too young.

HOW WAS HE A HARD WORKER?

proof from story

Buffalo Bill

HOW WAS HE BOLD?

proof from story

HOW WAS HE HONEST?

proof from story

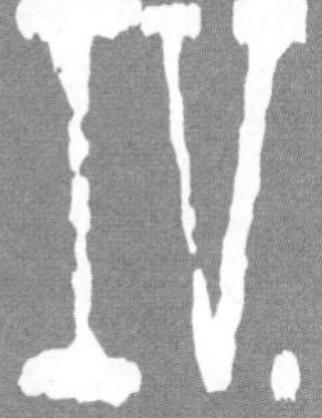

WRITE

Write a **letter** to a friend explaining why you think Buffalo Bill will make a good Pony Express rider.

1. Tell your friend about what kind of person Buffalo Bill is. Use the web on page 132.
2. Use the Writers' Checklist to edit your letter.

Continue writing your letter on the next page.

Continue your letter below.

WRITERS' CHECKLIST

Capitalization

- ☐ **In the heading, did you use a comma between the city and the state?** EXAMPLE: *Fort Laramie, Wyoming*
- ☐ **Did you use a comma between the date and the year?** EXAMPLE: *May 4, 1860*

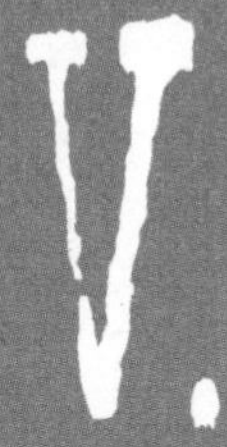

V. LOOK BACK

What made *Buffalo Bill and the Pony Express* easy or hard to read? Write your answer here.

Think about Your Reading

READERS' CHECKLIST

Ease

- ☐ **Was the reading easy to read?**
- ☐ **Were you able to read it smoothly?**

13

Tomás and the Library Lady

What if you have no TV or computers? What could you do? You could sit and listen to the stories others tell. You could also tell stories about your life.

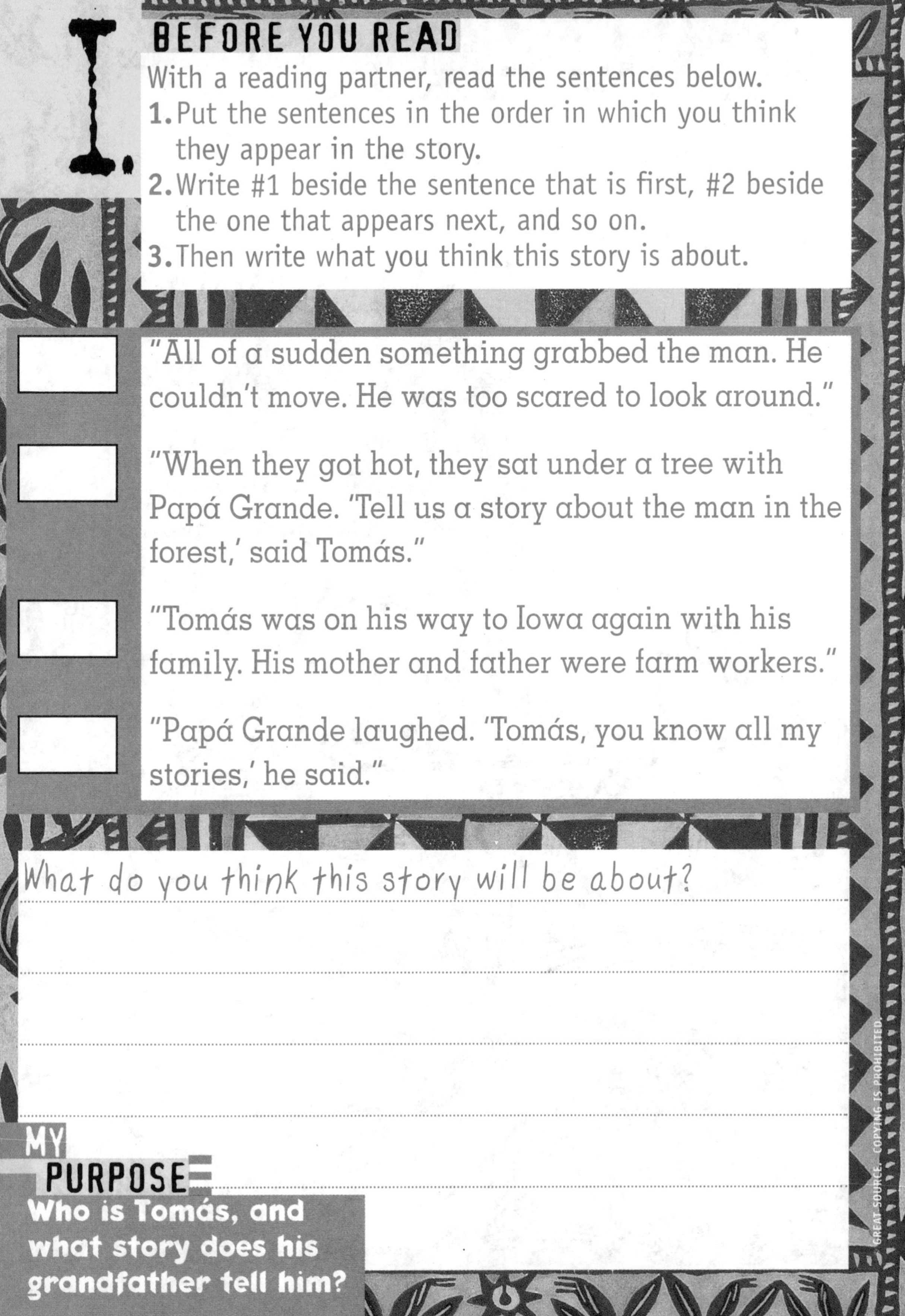

I. BEFORE YOU READ

With a reading partner, read the sentences below.

1. Put the sentences in the order in which you think they appear in the story.
2. Write #1 beside the sentence that is first, #2 beside the one that appears next, and so on.
3. Then write what you think this story is about.

☐ "All of a sudden something grabbed the man. He couldn't move. He was too scared to look around."

☐ "When they got hot, they sat under a tree with Papá Grande. 'Tell us a story about the man in the forest,' said Tomás."

☐ "Tomás was on his way to Iowa again with his family. His mother and father were farm workers."

☐ "Papá Grande laughed. 'Tomás, you know all my stories,' he said."

What do you think this story will be about?

MY PURPOSE

Who is Tomás, and what story does his grandfather tell him?

READ

Read this part of *Tomás and the Library Lady*.

1. First, read and circle anything that happens to Tomás.
2. Then, read the story again. In the Notes, **draw** pictures of what you see in your mind.

Tomás and the Library Lady
by Pat Mora

Response Notes

It was midnight. The light of the full moon followed the tired old car. Tomás was tired too. Hot and tired. He missed his own bed, in his own house in Texas.

EXAMPLE:

Tomás was on his way to Iowa again with his family. His mother and father were farm workers. They picked fruit and vegetables for Texas farmers in the winter and for Iowa farmers

Texas (Tex•as)—state in the southern United States.
Iowa (I•o•wa)—state in the middle of the United States.

Response Notes

in the summer. Year after year they <u>bump-bumped</u> along in their rusty old car. "Mamá," whispered Tomás, "if I had a glass of cold water, I would drink it in large gulps. I would suck the ice. I would pour the last drops of water on my face."

DOUBLE-ENTRY JOURNAL

Quote	What I Think About It
"Year after year they bump-bumped along in their rusty old car."	

Tomás was glad when the car finally stopped. He helped his grandfather, Papá Grande, climb down. Tomás said, "*Buenas noches*"—"Good night"

bump-bumped—moved with bumps and jolts.

Response Notes

TOMÁS AND THE LIBRARY LADY
(continued)

—to Papá, Mamá, Papá Grande, and to his little brother, Enrique. He curled up on the cot in the small house that his family shared with the other workers.

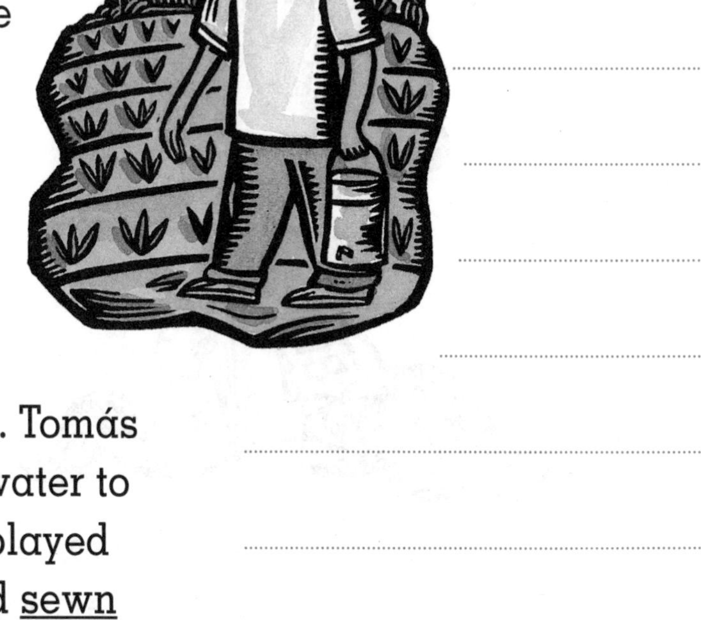

Early the next morning Mamá and Papá went out to pick corn in the green fields. All day they worked in the hot sun. Tomás and Enrique carried water to them. Then the boys played with a ball Mamá had sewn from an old teddy bear.

DOUBLE-ENTRY JOURNAL

Quote	What I Think About It
"All day they worked in the hot sun."	

sewn—made with needle and thread.
cot—small bed.

Response Notes

When they got hot, they sat under a tree with Papá Grande.

"Tell us the story about the man in the forest," said Tomás.

Tomás liked to listen to Papá Grande tell stories in Spanish. Papá Grande was the best storyteller in the family.

"En un tiempo pasado," Papá Grande began. "Once upon a time . . . on a windy night a man was riding a horse through a forest. The wind was howling, *whoooooooo*, and the leaves were blowing, *whish, whish* . . .

"All of a sudden something grabbed the man. He couldn't move. He was too scared to look around. All night long he wanted to ride away. But he couldn't.

DOUBLE-ENTRY JOURNAL

Quote	What I Think About It
"All night long he	
wanted to ride away.	
But he couldn't."	

TOMÁS AND THE LIBRARY LADY
(continued)

Response Notes

"How the wind howled, *whoooooooo*. How the leaves blew. How his teeth chattered!

"Finally the sun came up. Slowly the man turned around. And who do you think was holding him?"

Tomás smiled and said, "A thorny tree."

howled—screamed.
chattered (chat•tered)—hit against each other because of the cold.
thorny (thorn•y)—sharp and prickly.

Response Notes

Papá Grande laughed. "Tomás, you know all my stories," he said. "There are many more in the library. You are big enough to go by yourself. Then you can teach us new stories."

DOUBLE-ENTRY JOURNAL

Quote	What I Think About It
"'Tomás, you know all my stories,' he said. 'There are many more in the library.'"	

reread

Reread *Tomás and the Library Lady*. Think about the story Tomás's grandfather tells. Be sure you have written how you feel about each quote in the **Double-entry Journals**.

WORD WORK

A **compound word** is a long word made from 2 small words.

1. Circle 3 compound words in these sentences from *Tomás and the Library Lady*.
2. Then write the words on the chart. An example has been done for you.

- "You are big enough to go by yourself."
- "He helped his grandfather, Papá Grande, climb down."
- "Papá Grande was the best storyteller in the family."

Compound Word	Small Word	Small Word
1. yourself	your	self
2.		
3.		

Below is a box of small words. Put them together to make 3 new compound words.

book	top	board	case	hill	snow

1.

2.

3.

READING REMINDER

Make pictures in your mind of what you're reading about. It will help you remember and enjoy a story's plot and characters.

GET READY TO WRITE

PREWRITE

Plan a new ending to *Tomás and the Library Lady*.

1. Use the Story Chart below to plan another story Papá Grande might tell Tomás.
2. Use the Story Chart to plan your new ending.

SETTING

Where and when the story takes place

CHARACTER

Who the character is

PROBLEM

What problem the character has

THE ENDING

How the character solves the problem

IV. WRITE

Write a new **story ending** to *Tomás and the Library Lady*.

1. Use your plan on page 144.
2. Start with Tomás's words: "Tell us the story about...."
3. Use the Writers' Checklist to edit your story.

"Tell us the story about

Continue writing your story ending on the next page.

Continue your story ending below.

WRITERS' CHECKLIST

Apostrophes

☐ **Did you use an apostrophe (') followed by an s to show ownership or possession of singular words?** EXAMPLES: *Tomás's bed, Papá Grande's story, the tree's branches.*

LOOK BACK

What part of *Tomás and the Library Lady* did you like the most? Write your answer below.

Think about Your Reading

READERS' CHECKLIST

Enjoyment

☐ **Did you like the reading?**

☐ **Would you recommend the reading to a friend?**

14

Going Home

Have you ever taken a trip to your parents' childhood home? Have you ever been away from your own home for a long time? How did you feel? How was it different?

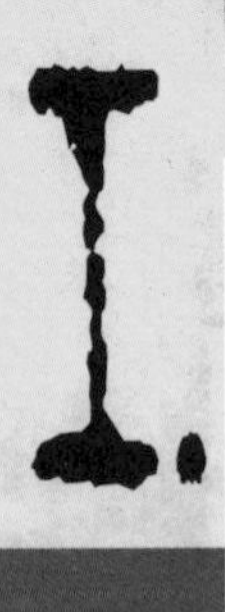

BEFORE YOU READ

Read the title *Going Home*. Think about what it will be about.

1. Then read each of the sentences below.
2. Put an *X* by those you think might happen in the story.

☐ We forgot to put our suitcases into the back of our old station wagon.

☐ Almost everyone in the camp has come to see us off.

☐ It is a long drive to our parents' village of La Perla.

☐ On our trip to Mexico, we sailed around the world.

MY PURPOSE

Where did the family go, and what happened on the way there?

II. READ

Read this part of the story *Going Home*.

1. When you read the first time, underline details about where the family is going and what happens to them.
2. Then, read the story again. This time, **connect** Carlos's trip with his family to a trip you have taken. Write your ideas in the Notes.

Going Home by Eve Bunting

"We are going home, Carlos," Mama says, hugging me.

She sparkles with excitement. "Home is here," she says. "But it is there, too."

She and Papa are happy. My sisters and I are not so sure. Mexico is not our home, though we were born there.

Papa piles our boxes and suitcases into the back of our old station wagon. He slides in our battered cooler, which is filled with food and cold drinks for the journey. My little sister, Nora, and my big sister, Dolores, get into the back seat with me. Nora is five, Dolores is ten.

Papa locks the door to our

sparkles (spark•les)—shines.
battered (bat•tered)—worn; old and used.

Response Notes

EXAMPLE:

My neighbors were also born in Mexico.

Response Notes

house. The house really belongs to Mr. Culloden, the <u>labor</u> manager, but it is ours as long as we work the crops for him. It has been ours for almost five years.

STORY CHART

Setting	Characters
Where and when does the story take place?	Who are the characters?

Almost everyone in the camp has come out to see us off.

Nora waves to her best friend, Maria.

"Don't be sad, Norita," Dolores says. "We are only going for Christmas. You will see Maria again soon."

We're on our way!

labor (lab•or)—work group.

Going Home (continued)

Response Notes

It is a long drive to our parents' village of La Perla, and we are a little nervous as we cross the border into Mexico.

"Are you sure they will let us back, Papa?" I ask.

"Of course. Do not worry. We are legal farm workers. We have our papeles."

"Papers, Papa," I say quickly.

"Sí. Papeles." Papa speaks always in Spanish. He and Mama have no English. There is no need for it in the fields. But I'm always trying to teach them.

STORY CHART

Where is the family going?

Now we are in Mexico.

I see no difference, but Mama does.

"Mexico! Mexico!" She blows kisses at the sun-filled winter sky.

nervous (ner•vous)—worried.

Response Notes

Every night Mama and my sisters sleep in the car. Papa and I lie on the ground, wrapped in blankets. I look up at the stars.

"Is it really nice in La Perla?" I ask.

"Yes, Mijo," Papa says. "The village is small, of course."

"You've told us how pretty it is," I say.

"Yes." I feel him smile in the dark. "Pretty."

Mijo (mi•ho)—In Spanish, mijo is short for "mi hijo," which means "my son."

STORY CHART

How do the parents feel about Mexico?

reread

Reread *Going Home*. Be sure you have answered all the **Story Chart** questions.

WORD WORK

Study each word in the box.

1. Put words that end in silent *e* in the first column.
2. Put words that end in 2 consonants in the second column.

home	crops	work
drive	ground	smile

Silent e Words	Words Ending in 2 Consonants
home	ground

3. Now choose 4 of the words. Add *–s* or *–es* and *–ing* to each word.

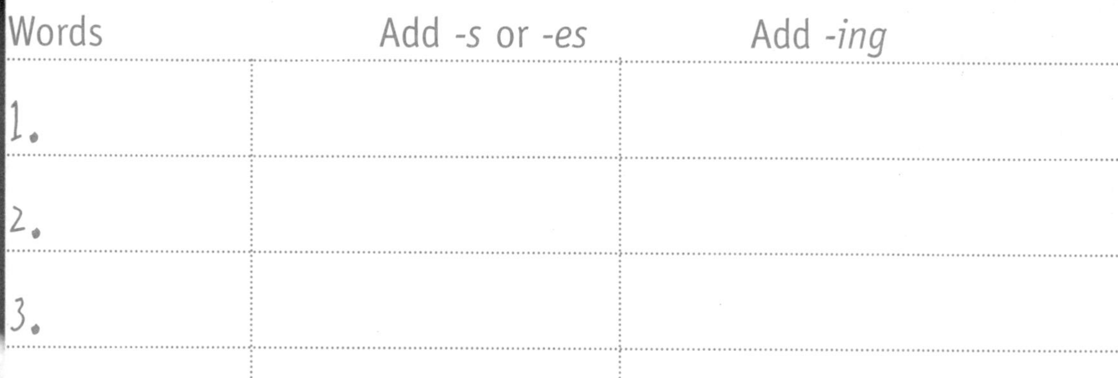

Words	Add *-s* or *-es*	Add *-ing*
1.		
2.		
3.		
4.		

READING REMINDER

Making connections between a story and your own life helps keep you interested in what you're reading.

GET READY TO WRITE

WRITE DETAILS

Get ready to write a poem about a place you think of as home.

1. Write your topic in the box marked "My Topic."
2. In the spaces, brainstorm details that relate to your senses.
3. Write at least 2 details in each space.

SIGHT

HEARING

MY TOPIC

TASTE

SMELL

TOUCH

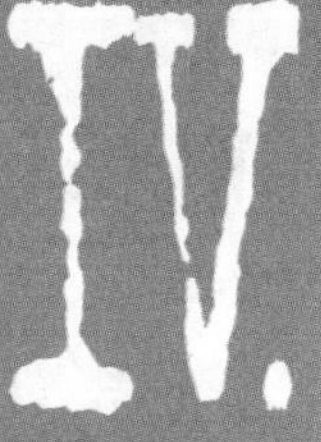

WRITE

Write a **poem**.

1. Use your ideas from page 154 to get started.
2. Give your poem a title.
3. Begin by completing the sentence below. Use a new sentence for each of the 5 senses.
4. Use the Writers' Checklist to revise your poem.

Title:

Home is where

Continue writing on the next page.

Continue your poem.

WRITERS' CHECKLIST

Apostrophes

☐ **Did you add an apostrophe (') to show ownership or possession of a plural word that ends in *s*?**

EXAMPLES: *many trees' leaves, babies' cries, ladies' gloves*

V. LOOK BACK

What 2 things made this story easy or hard to read? Write your answer below.

Think about Your Reading

READERS' CHECKLIST

Ease

☐ **Was the reading easy to read?**

☐ **Were you able to read it smoothly?**

Fox and Crane

What would happen if you invited a friend to dinner and served food your friend could not eat? Find out what happens to the friendship of Fox and Crane in this story.

BEFORE YOU READ

Read the sentences below from the fable "Fox and Crane."

1. Think about which sentence comes first, second, third, and fourth.
2. With a reading partner, number the sentences in the order you think they will appear in the fable.
3. Then make a prediction about "Fox and Crane."

☐ "When Fox arrived, Crane had made a very delicious soup."

☐ "Crane accepted the invitation, and Fox made some porridge and spread it out on plates."

☐ "Fox was angry. Crane had given her tit for tat."

☐ "But Crane put his long beak in the jar and relished every drop of his wonderful soup."

What do you think will happen in this fable?

....

....

....

....

....

....

MY PURPOSE

What is the lesson of this fable?

II. READ

Read "Fox and Crane."

1. As you read it the first time, underline parts that have to do with the lesson the fable teaches.
2. On the second reading, write in your Notes any **questions** that pop into your head about Fox or Crane and their friendship.

"Fox and Crane"
by Patricia Polacco

Response Notes

Fox and Crane were friends. One day Fox invited Crane for dinner. Crane accepted the invitation, and Fox made some porridge and spread it out on plates.

Crane pecked and pecked at the plate with his long beak.

"Eat it up, Brother Crane," said Fox. "It's so very good—I made it myself."

Crane watched as Fox licked her plate clean. Crane pecked and pecked, but could not get anything off the plate.

EXAMPLE: Does Fox see that Crane is having trouble eating?

invited (in•**vit**•ed)—asked.
accepted (ac•**cept**•ed)—said yes to.
porridge (**por**•ridge)—hot cereal.
pecked—hit with his beak.

"Wasn't that a lovely dinner!" Fox exclaimed. "But you did not eat, my brother."

STOP AND RETELL **stop and retell** STOP AND RETELL

What happened at Fox's dinner?

STOP AND THINK STOP AND THINK STOP AND THINK

Crane sat silent, but then answered: "Sister Fox, I would be pleased if you could come to my house for dinner tomorrow night."

When Fox arrived, Crane had made a very delicious soup. He served the soup in tall jars with very narrow necks.

"Eat it up, Sister Fox. It's so

necks—openings.
pleased—happy.
arrived (ar•rived)—got there.
narrow (nar•row)—skinny.

Response Notes

very good—I made it myself."

Fox looked and looked at the jar. She turned it this way and turned it that way. She barked at it, she sniffed at it, but not a drop of soup could she get, for her head was too big to go into the long neck of the jar. She couldn't tip the jar, for she could not hold it with her paws.

barked—made a loud noise.
sniffed—smelled.
paws—animal feet.

Response Notes

But Crane put his long beak in the jar and relished every drop of his wonderful soup.

Fox was angry. Crane had given her tit for tat. But they valued their friendship, and from that time on, at each of their tables there was always a plate and always a jar.

relished (rel•ished)—enjoyed.
given her tit for tat—gotten even; given her what she deserved.

STOP AND RETELL stop and retell STOP AND RETELL

What happened at Crane's dinner?

reread

Reread "Fox and Crane." Try to restate in your own words the lesson about life that the fable teaches. Be sure you have answered the **Stop and Think** questions.

WORD WORK

"Fox and Crane" has many long words. You can read them if you follow these tips:

- Take off each suffix.
- Read the small word.
- Then say the small word and the suffix.

1. Fill in the chart below.
2. Cross out the suffix.
3. Write the small word under the heading "Base Word."

Word from Story	Base Word
1. arrived	arrive
2. valued	
3. sniffed	
4. relished	
5. answered	

READING REMINDER

The animal characters in fables often teach an important lesson about life.

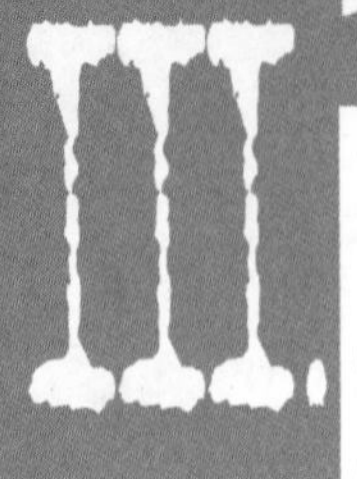

GET READY TO WRITE

CREATE AN ENDING

Complete the chart below about "Fox and Crane." Think of a new ending for the fable.

Setting Where and when does the fable take place?

Fox's Problem What is Fox's problem?

Crane's Problem What is Crane's problem?

Ending How does the fable end?

Lesson What did you learn?

Your New Ending What is your new ending?

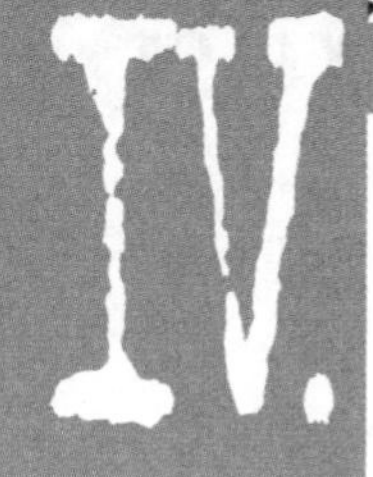

IV. WRITE

Write a new **story ending** for "Fox and Crane."

1. Use the ideas from page 164.
2. Start your new ending after the sentence, "Fox was angry."
3. Use the Writers' Checklist to edit your story.

Continue your story on the next page.

Continue your story ending below.

WRITERS' CHECKLIST

Apostrophes

☐ **Did you add an apostrophe and an s ('s) to plural nouns that don't end in s to show ownership or possession?**
EXAMPLES: *men's books, people's cars, deer's hooves*

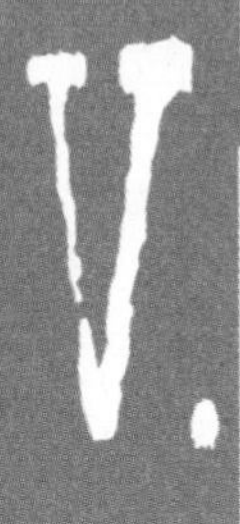

LOOK BACK

What did you learn about friendship from reading "Fox and Crane?" Write your answer below.

Think about Your Reading

READERS' CHECKLIST

Understanding

☐ **Did you understand the reading?**

☐ **Can you tell a friend what the reading is about?**

16

Abuela

Do you know your grandmother or any older women? What is she like? What does she do? What does she say? What sort of things does she teach you?

I. BEFORE YOU READ

The word *abuela* (a•bue•la) in Spanish means "grandma." The next story is about a girl and her *abuela*. Take a minute to think about grandmas.

1. In the web below, write ideas about your grandma or an older woman who spends time with you.
2. Then share your ideas with a partner.

Places we go

What we do together

Why I love her

Grandma or Older Woman

What she teaches

How she looks

What she's like

MY PURPOSE

What is the grandmother in the story like?

II. READ

Read this part of the book *Abuela*.

1. As you read, circle details about Abuela that show what she is like.
2. On your next reading, use your imagination to **draw** pictures in the Notes of what Abuela does.

Abuela by Arthur Dorros

Response Notes

Abuela takes me on the bus. We go all around the city.

Abuela is my grandma. She is my mother's mother. *Abuela* means "grandma" in Spanish. Abuela speaks mostly Spanish because that's what people spoke where she grew up, before she came to this country. Abuela and I are always going places.

Today we're going to the park. *"El parque es lindo,"* says Abuela. I know what she means. I think the park is beautiful too.

"Tantos pájaros," Abuela says as a flock of birds surrounds us. So many birds. They're picking at the bread we brought.

What if they picked me up, and carried me high above the

flock—group of animals that travels together.

Response Notes

park? What if I could fly? Abuela would wonder where I was.

Swooping like a bird, I'd call to her.

DOUBLE-ENTRY JOURNAL

Quote	Your Thoughts About It
"What if I could fly? Abuela would wonder where I was."	

Then she'd see me flying. Rosalba the bird.

"*Rosalba el pájaro,*" she'd say.

"*Ven, Abuela.* Come, Abuela," I'd say. "*Si, quiero volar,*" Abuela would reply as she leaped into the sky with her skirt flapping in the wind.

leaped—jumped.
flapping (flap•ping**)**—moving and swinging.

reread

Look back over *Abuela* one more time. Think about what Abuela is like and be sure to respond to the **Double-entry Journal** quote.

WORD WORK

You can make a small word longer by adding **prefixes** to the beginning and **suffixes** at the end.

1. Make the words in the chart longer.
2. Use the prefixes and suffixes in the box to make these small words into bigger words.

Prefixes:	Suffixes:
pre-, re-, un	**-ing, -ed, -ful, -er**

Small Word	Bigger Word
1. go + suffix	going
2. pick + suffix	
3. swoop + suffix	
4. prefix + view	
5. wonder + suffix	
6. soar + suffix	
7. prefix + take	
8. prefix + able	

READING REMINDER

Use your imagination to help you get an idea of what characters are like.

GET READY TO WRITE

THINK ABOUT CHARACTERS

Get ready to write a paragraph that describes.

1. Think about how the story shows what kind of a person Abuela is. Ideas that describe what a person is like are called **character traits**.
2. For each character trait below, give an example from the story. One example is done for you.

CHARACTER CHART

Character Trait:	Character Trait:
fun Example:	thoughtful Example: brings bread for the birds in the park

Abuela

Character Trait:	Character Trait:
enjoys nature Example:	loving Example:

IV. WRITE

Write a **paragraph** that describes Abuela.

1. Use your character chart on page 172 for ideas.
2. Begin with the topic sentence below. End with a closing sentence that tells how you feel about Abuela.
3. Use the Writers' Checklist to edit your paragraph.

Title:

When Rosalba grows up, she will be like her grandmother.

Continue writing your paragraph on the next page.

Continue writing your paragraph below.

WRITERS' CHECKLIST

Capitalization

☐ **Did you use a capital letter for the names of particular people?** EXAMPLE: *Abuela Rosalba*

LOOK BACK

What did you learn from reading *Abuela*? Write your answer below.

Think about Your Reading

READERS' CHECKLIST

Meaning

☐ **Did you learn something from the reading?**

☐ **Did you have a strong feeling about one part of the reading?**

Acknowledgements

6 "Shooting Stars" From Always Wondering by Aileen Fisher. Copyright © 1991 Aileen Fisher. Used by permission of Marian Reiner for the author.

7 "First Moon Landing" by J. Patrick Lewis. Reprinted by permission of the author.

8 "The Moon" by Lillian Fisher, reprinted by permission of the author

9 "Song" by Ashley Bryan. Copyright © 1992 by Ashley Bryan. Used by permission of HarperCollins Publishers.

13 From Play Ball, Amelia Bedelia by Margaret Parish. Text copyright © 1992 by Margaret Parish. Pictures copyright © 1972 by Wallace Tripp. Used by permission of HarperCollins Publishers

23 "Winter Morning" by Ogden Nash. Copyright © 1962 by Ogden Nash. Reprinted by permission of Curtis Brown, Ltd.

24 "Go Wind" From I Feel the Same Way by Lilian Moore. Copyright © 1967, 1995 Lilian Moore. Used by permission of Marian Reiner.

25 "Mister Sun" by J. Patrick Lewis. Reprinted by permission of the author.

33 From Frogs by Laura Driscoll, copyright © 1998 by Laura Driscoll. Used by permission of Grosset & Dunlap, an imprint of Penguin Putnam Books for Young Readers, a division of Penguin Putnam Inc.

43 From I'll Catch the Moon by Nina Crews. Copyright © 1996 by Nina Crews. Used by permission of HarperCollins Publishers.

53 From Volcanoes: Mountains That Blow Their Tops by Nicholas Nirgiotis, copyright © 1996 by Nicholas Nirgiotis. Used by permission of Grosset & Dunlap, an imprint of Penguin Putnam Books for Young Readers, a division of Penguin Putnam Inc.

63 From Cave People by Linda Hayword, copyright © 1997 by Linda Hayword, text. Used by permission of Grosset & Dunlap, an imprint of Penguin Books for Young Readers, a division of Penguin Putnam Inc.

71 From Look at Your Eyes by Paul Showers. Copyright © 1992 by Paul Showers. Used by permission of HarperCollins Publishers.

79 From Just a Few Words, Mr. Lincoln by Jean Fritz, text copyright © 1993 by Jean Fritz. Used by permission of Grosset & Dunlap, an imprint of Penguin Putnam Books for Young Readers, a division of Penguin Putnam Inc.

91 From Why I Sneeze, Shiver, Hiccup, and Yawn by Melvin Berger. Text copyright © 1983 by Melvin Berger. Used by permission of HarperCollins Publishers.

103 From MARVIN REDPOST: ALONE IN HIS TEACHER'S HOUSE by Louis Sachar. Copyright ©1994 by Louis Sachar. Reprinted by permission of Random House Children's Books, a division of Random House, Inc.

117 From HUNGRY, HUNGRY SHARKS by Joanna Cole Copyright © 1986 by Joanna Cole. Reprinted by permission of Random House Children's Books, a division of Random House, Inc.

127 From Buffalo Bill and the Pony Express by Eleanor Coerr. Text copyright © 1995 by Eleanor Coerr. Illustration copyright © 1995 by Dan Bolognese. Used by permission of HarperCollins Publishers.

137 From TOMAS AND THE LIBRARY LADY by Pat Mora. Text copyright ©1997 by Pat Mora. Reprinted by permission of Alfred A. Knopf Children's Books, a division of Random House, Inc.

147 From Going Home by Eve Bunting. Text copyright © 1996 by Edward D. Bunting and Anne E. Bunting. Trustees of the Edward D. Bunting and Anne E. Bunting Family Trust. Illustrations copyright © 1996 by David Diaz. Photographs by Cecelia Zieba-Diaz. Used by permission of HarperCollins Publishers.

159 "Fox and Crane", from Babushka's Mother Goose by Patricia Polacco, copyright © 1995 by Patricia Polacco. Used by permission of Philomel Books, an imprint of Penguin Putnam Books for Young Readers, a division of Penguin Putnam Inc.

169 From ABUELA by Arthur Dorros, copyright © 1991 by Arthur Dorros. Used by permission of Dutton Children's Books, a division of Penguin Putnam Inc.

Cover Photography:
All photos © Eileen Ryan.

Illustration:
Active Reader: Johanna Hantel
Chapter Two: Louise Baker
Chapter Three: Bradley Clark
Chapter Five: Mike Dammer
Chapter Six: Phyllis Pollema-Cahill
Chapter Seven: Steve Boswick
Chapter Eight: Rich Stergulz
Chapter Nine: Victor Kennedy
Chapter Ten: Bill Peterson
Chapter Eleven: Reggie Holladay
Chapter Twelve: Tim Jones
Chapter Thirteen: Patti Green
Chapter Sixten: Donna Perrone

Cover and Book Design:
Christine Ronan, Sean O'Neill, and Maria Mariottini, Ronan Design

Permissions:
Feldman and Associates

Developed by Nieman Inc.

The editors have made every effort to trace the ownership of all copyrighted selections found in this book and to make full acknowledgment for their use. Omissions brought to our attention will be corrected in a subsequent edition.

Author/Title **Index**